Father ten Boom

God's Man

BY CORRIE TEN BOOM WITH JOHN AND
        ELIZABETH SHERRILL
  The Hiding Place
BY CORRIE TEN BOOM WITH JAMIE BUCKINGHAM
  Tramp for the Lord
BY CORRIE TEN BOOM WITH C. C. CARLSON
  In My Father's House
BY CORRIE TEN BOOM
  Corrie's Christmas Memories
  Corrie ten Boom's Prison Letters
  He Cares, He Comforts—JESUS IS VICTOR
  Each New Day
  He Sets the Captive Free—JESUS IS VICTOR
  Father ten Boom—God's Man

Father ten Boom

GOD'S MAN

CORRIE TEN BOOM

Fleming H. Revell Company
Old Tappan, New Jersey

Library of Congress Cataloging in Publication Data

Ten Boom, Corrie.
    Father ten Boom, God's man

    1. Boom, Casper ten, 1859-1944.   2.   Reformed (Reformed Church) in the Netherlands—Biography.
3.   Haarlem—Biography.   I.   Title.
BX9479.B56T46   284'.2492   [B]   78-18713
ISBN 0-8007-0958-6

To Walter Gastil

who went home to be with the Lord the week I finished this book. Walter Gastil had been a close friend and advisor. He had seen some of the material in the book and wrote about it: "I believe that the Casper ten Boom story is greatly needed. The whole world needs to be brought back to a love for God; strong family ties, love for each other, and fellowship within the church.

"The Casper ten Boom household, of which Casper was the head and priest, was a shining example of all these characteristics. That family started with two individuals becoming a partnership, each doing his or her part and neither abdicating—above all, working together with mutual respect, consideration, and love. Now is the time to tell the blessing of such homes as the basis of our civilization and the heart of national strength."

Remember the days of long ago! Ask your father and the aged men; They will tell you all about it.

Deuteronomy 32:7 LB

Contents

Oh, God Jehovah, good and kind,
On Zion's mount in clouds enshrined,
Thou art our sun and shield forever.
To upright souls that seek Thy face
Thou givest glory, truth and grace;
E'en in death's vale Thou failest never.
O Lord of hosts, how blest is he
Who puts his stedfast trust in Thee!

See Psalm 84

1

My Last Good-bye

"The Lord be with you, Father."

"And with your spirit, child."

Those were the last words Father and I exchanged after the many years we had lived so happily together. I was standing in the corridor of a prison. Because of his age, Father had been permitted to sit on a chair. A long row of prisoners stood nearby, their faces turned to the dirty yellow wall. In this line were all of Father's children, three daughters and a son, and Peter, one of his grandsons.

Peter described it this way:

The long hours crept by slowly as we stood there facing that yellow brick wall. My heart was full of questions. I kept thinking of the Psalm which Grandfather had read the evening before. After our imprisonment we had been taken to the police station at Haarlem. In the gymnasium there, with thirty other prisoners lying and sitting on the floor around him, Grandfather had taken his Bible and read the Ninety-first Psalm. How peaceful those words had sounded to our anxious souls: "He that dwelleth in the secret place of the most High shall abide under the shadow of the Almighty. I will say of the Lord, He is my refuge and my fortress: my God; in him will I trust."

10

But now, standing in the corridor of Scheveningen prison, doubt filled my heart. "A thousand shall fall at thy side," Grandfather had read, "and ten thousand at thy right hand; but it shall not come nigh thee."

But tragedy *had* struck. Where was the host of angels we had prayed for so often? Had God forgotten us? Then I glanced over at Grandfather sitting in the corner. There was such an expression of peace on his pale face that I could not help marveling. He actually *was* protected. God had built a fence around him. Suddenly I knew: The everlasting arms are around all of us. God does not make mistakes. He is at the controls.

At last they took me to my cell. As I walked past Grandfather, I stopped, bent over him, and kissed him good-bye. He looked up at me and said, "My boy, are we not a privileged generation?"

Those were his last words to me.

Today, as I remember this event after more than thirty years, I have a thousand more reasons to say, "Yes, Grandfather, we *are* a privileged generation!"

No one was allowed to speak. The cadence of the steps of heavily armed soldiers and an occasional roughly shouted command were the only sounds. Far away, I heard a prisoner suddenly pound on the door of his cell with his fists, crying, "Let me out! Open this door!" The corridor smelled damp, like an insufficiently aired cellar.

"The Lord be with you, Father."

The thought came to my mind: Shall I try to ask him to give me a quick blessing? No, it is not necessary. I have received his blessing through all the years we have been together.

I felt a shove on my back.

"Move on! Hurry up! Hurry up!" said the guard as he
jerked me toward my cell. That was the last time I saw
Father. At that moment, something in me broke which took
a long time to heal.

Designs and Patterns

Let me tell you who Father was, what kind of man he
was. I am eighty-five years of age now, one year older than
Father was when he died in prison. I have a good memory,
and I have listened to many people talk about my father.

Peter, the nephew who was in prison with us, recently
discovered an old chest, filled with many letters and papers written by my parents and other ancestors. As I read
them, they strongly reinforced the knowledge and memories I have of my father. My, what a wealth of information!

Those papers made me understand how important all of
us are because of our influence on succeeding generations.
Did his forefathers influence Father to become the type of
man he was? In some ways, yes. God had a plan for
Father's life, and God used these relatives to mold Father
according to that plan.

You have different ancestors. Do not be discouraged and
think, "I can never be like Casper ten Boom." Casper was
Casper, you are you, and that is good!

An artist is able to create wonderful paintings, or tapes-
tries, or statues because of his gifts and his creative discipline. You may not have artistic talent, but you can learn
from studying the way the artist uses his gifts, and you can
apply his principles to your own special gifts.

I want to tell you about some of the designs and patterns
in Father's life. This will not make you a Casper ten Boom,
but it can help you become the person God has planned that

you should be. The same God who made Father a blessing can make you a blessing.

Paul prayed that the Colossians would see things from God's point of view. I pray that the Lord will make it possible for you to see the ten Boom family history from God's point of view.

Gift of the Spirit

When I first came to the United States, I was often embarrassed at the flattering way people introduced me. I would respond by telling them the story of a woodpecker who tapped with his beak against the trunk of a tree, as woodpeckers do. At that same moment, lightning struck the tree and destroyed it. The woodpecker flew away and said to the other birds, "I did not know that there was so much power in my beak."

Privileged by God, Casper did the work. How wrong it would be to say, "What a good job Casper ten Boom did!" No, it was not the woodpecker—it was the lightning. It was not Casper—it was the Lord.

Did Father have great faith? I don't know, but I do know he had faith in a great God. Jesus said that even if our faith is as small as a mustard seed, it can move mountains. It is not the quantity of faith that is important, but the quality. Father's faith was strong because the Holy Spirit gave it to him. The Holy Spirit is willing to give such faith to everyone who surrenders to God and prays that He will fill his heart.

But the fruit of the Spirit is love, joy, peace, longsuffering, gentleness, goodness, faith, Meekness, temperance . . . .

Galatians 5:22, 23

Father was filled with the fruit of the Spirit, and that is why he was an outstanding man. This is true of any man whose life bears the fruit of the Holy Spirit. He will always stand out, wherever he is—in the tiny corner of the earth where Father lived out his life, or on the center stage of the world. What wonderful fruit! Fruit that makes the world hungry—salt that makes the world thirsty!

Father knew that he was simply God's handiwork—a happy tool in God's hands. His motto was *Soli Deo gloria*—to God alone the glory. The same God who created and guided Father is willing to be your heavenly Father. To those who receive Jesus, He gives the right to become children of God.

Discoveries in the Old Chest

Somebody once asked me, "Do you know anything about your background? Your story interests me. The ten Booms seem to have had faith in the Bible, love for the Jews, vision for where there was need, and willingness to help."

I found much of my family background in the many letters from the old chest Peter found. They contain our whole family story, which I would like to share.

I am sitting in my easy chair. Peter is sitting cross-legged on the floor, with the open chest between us. It is as if we can reach back into the past. Old papers have a certain curious musty smell. As we remove the neat little stacks and finger the yellowed sheets, we notice the different styles of handwriting. Some are curly (and rounded), others are straight (and angular), some are scrawled so small that it takes a magnifying glass to decipher them. Yes, different kinds of handwriting have personalities, too!

Here are letters written by my father's parents and

When Corrie and her nephew Peter read the letters in the old chest they discovered much of their Christian family heritage.

grandparents, and letters written by me many years ago. There are Father's notebooks, with memories, illustrations, and stories he used in his talks. Here is a diary, which Mother kept for twenty-five years, and in which she wrote about her children.

These yellowed pages bring back many memories. In some small way, I am living my life over again; that rich life with Father and Mother, the training ground of my ministry today. There was so much music, fun, love, and faith. One of Father's favorite songs was:

> *'k Zal gedenken hoe voor dezen*
> *Ons de Heer heeft gunst bewezen.*
> I will remember how in days gone by
> God cared for us and showed us His love.

When we dig up the gold of the past, it must be beaten into useful coins for today. Past, present, and future belong together. The most joyful knowledge is that we are citizens of heaven. Our outlook goes beyond this world, and we are in training for eternity.

Recently, a friend said to me, "Do you know what I like about getting older? One discovers something of the plan behind the happenings of the past. When we look back, we realize that behind many events, which were not important in themselves, there is a design, an order, a continuity."

2

Gerrit ten Boom
1760–1839

I remember particularly one evening when I was a child. We were sitting around the oval table, on one of those special occasions when time seemed to stand still in the Beje. Father had just closed the copper hinges of the Bible after his evening reading.

That day, we did not run away to play, as we usually did after the Bible reading at the close of our meals, for Father had promised to tell us about his grandfather. I removed the dishes and put the black and red cloth back over the table. We heard the clip-clop of the horse-drawn streetcar in the Barteljorisstraat, and the chimes of the carillon on the Grote Kerk nearby resounded over the rooftops with "A Mighty Fortress is Our God."

"A mighty fortress. Yes, that is what God is for us, and what He was for our forefathers," said my father, wrapping his hand around his beard, as he often did when he was deep in thought.

"In 1816, when he was fifty-six years old, my grandfather Gerrit's wife gave birth to their first child. It was a boy, and, of course, they gave him the name Willem."

"Why do you say *of course*, Father?"

"Willem was the name of all the princes of Orange who had reigned over Holland for centuries. Our family dearly loved the House of Orange.

18

"Your great-grandfather Gerrit was quite a good gardener, so you may wonder, children, why his son Willem chose another trade."

Father smiled. "God sometimes uses little events to change the direction of one's life. My grandfather Gerrit was the chief gardener of a large estate in Heemstede, a few miles from here. The name of that estate was Hofstede, Bronstede, Heemstede. Grandfather was proud of the petunias and tulips he produced in his rich landlord's garden.

"The owner's little daughter loved to play in the garden, and one day she pranced and danced right across the petunia beds, destroying the results of Grandfather's hard work in just a few minutes. The little rascal saw how annoyed he was and thought that rather interesting, so she did it again, several days in a row. Grandpa finally went to the landlord and told him what his naughty daughter had done.

"The landlord answered, 'Gerrit, the next time that happens, give the girl a good spanking. Go ahead—it will do her good.'

"Grandpa Gerrit did, indeed, spank the girl the next time she danced through the petunias. It worked, but she held an everlasting grudge against the strict gardener. When the landlord died, the girl was a young woman, the only heir to the estate. One of the first things she did was to fire my grandfather. The ten Boom family then moved to Haarlem. My grandfather started a business there, constructing and renting carriages."

It was fun to hear my father tell about his grandfather Gerrit. How we enjoyed that evening! It was as if we had taken a little walk with Father, right back into the past.

Cloud of Witnesses

In the old chest, we found a little notebook, in which my father had written more about his grandfather Gerrit.

March 27, 1927

Today I am starting a work which I have been planning to do for a long time, but for which I have not found time until now. It is my intention to put into writing some of the things I remember about my ancestors, and also to tell something of my own life.

I do this in order to glorify my Lord and Saviour. That is the most important thing, for I will pass away, and so will my children and grandchildren. We all live for a short time, but our Lord remains, and He is worthy to be honored, loved, and served by my descendants.

May these notes encourage the coming generations to serve the Lord and to walk in His ways. I know that a message like this from an ancestor can be an influence to that end, and I hope that many of those who live after me will get to know Him, whom to know is life eternal.

We are surrounded by a cloud of witnesses.

I am holding a pen in my hand. Its point is touching the paper and is putting into words the thoughts I am expressing. This pen represents the generations which were before me. I have the privilege of being the tip that touches the paper, the one who speaks to my generation, but I am united with my ancestors, those who shaped my life and whose blood flows through my veins.

Their lives were simple. They worked and prayed. They served God in the workshop, in the family, and in the church. Their homes, like the one behind my watch shop, were small circles where God's light could shine. They are the pen, of which I am the little tip running over the paper.

One hand holds us all. It is the hand of the One David meant when he wrote, "But the mercy of the Lord is from everlasting to everlasting upon them that fear him, and his righteousness unto children's children; To such as keep his covenant, and to those that remember his commandments to do them" (Psalms 103:17, 18).

How thankful I am for my courageous Christian grandfather, Gerrit ten Boom, who lived at the time of Napoleon. He was a deacon in the church, and a man of prayer, who suffered much from spiritual coldness in the church. The minister there preached such liberal ideas that he made the people's hair stand on end.

Once Grandfather Gerrit had to drive the minister to Haarlem after the church service in Heemstede. Grandfather had struggled with the liberal message in church that morning, which was bad enough, but when the minister suddenly said some appreciative words about Napoleon, Grandfather became very upset.

As they drove past the old houses and green gardens on either side of them, Grandfather took advantage of the long ride, and, as the horses' hooves kept time, told the minister what he thought about his unfaithfulness to the Bible and the Prince of Orange, which he had clearly demonstrated that morning. He showed the pastor the grave responsibility of putting his own philosophies above the Word of God.

The minister must have been impressed, because when they arrived in Haarlem, he stepped down from the carriage and said, "Well, Gerrit, next Sunday I will do better!"

"If God grants you the time to do so," was Grandfather's reply.

The minister died before the next Sunday arrived.

The Bible was the main literature in my great-grandfather Gerrit's house, although a few other small books on Christian subjects were preserved among his belongings. Their well-worn pages reveal the family's main interests.

One book, a thirty-two page, handwritten biography, *Life of the Godly and Blessed Petrus van der Velde (1758)*, was laboriously copied by Gerrit during the night between January 31 and February 1, 1804. I think he had borrowed the booklet and wanted it for himself.

Great-grandfather Gerrit's life was one of those seeds which was to bear fruit later. His home was referred to as a house of prayer. Thirty years after his death, the church in Heemstede became the scene of a new revival. Gerrit ten Boom's prayers and tears had not been in vain. The lessons of history often teach us patience.

3

Willem ten Boom
1816–1892

Willem, Gerrit's son, had just turned twelve when the family left the Bronstede estate and settled in the center of Haarlem. It must have been hard for the family to leave the beautiful green gardens of Bronstede and adapt to the busy street of a small town.

However, little Willem would never have made a good gardener. Small and slightly built, with crossed eyes, he was the opposite of his husky father. Willem's wife told her children that it took her years to decide whether Willem was looking at her or at somebody else. His father, Gerrit, had often tried to let Willem hold the reins when driving the horse-drawn carriage, but the poor fellow was so clumsy that his younger sister Cato had to take over.

A close relationship developed between Willem and Cato. They often wrote each other letters, some of which have been preserved. In these, they shared their inner struggles and doubts, their victories of faith, and their gratitude for God's goodness in their daily lives.

Soon after the family moved to Haarlem, a place was found for young Willem as an apprentice in a watch-repair shop. Until that time, Willem's education had been very limited, but by age twelve he had learned to read, write, and do arithmetic. In his generation, that was significant intellectual attainment.

24

My father noted, "I still have a few of my father's school books, and it is clear to me that he did not learn to read merely by means of the Bible and the Haarlem newspaper, as was customary in those days."

The beautiful handwriting and excellent style of his language, as found in letters from his adult years, tell us that he probably pursued his education on his own at every opportunity.

The year 1837 marked an important milestone in my grandfather Willem's life. With a working capital of one hundred guilders granted to him by his parents, twenty-one-year-old Willem opened his own watch shop in the Barteljorisstraat, Haarlem. The stage was set for the young watchmaker to marry and have his own family. When, four years later, he married Geertruide, he appeared to be moving toward a time of great prosperity. The business was growing. Watch owners in Haarlem often chose to have their timepieces repaired by the happy, well-dressed Mr. ten Boom.

Clouds and Sunshine on the Beje

Among the oldest letters found in the chest were some written by my grandfather, Willem ten Boom, to his sister Cato. Since their theme was usually the Lord, these letters tell us about the spiritual atmosphere in which my father grew up.

Their life was not easy. In the first fourteen years of their marriage, Geertruide gave birth to thirteen children, of which eight died at birth or at a very early age. Geertruide suffered from tuberculosis, and since the youngest child always slept in a crib at the foot of the bed, the infection was easily transmitted. On the death of one of the children, Willem wrote to his sister.

Dearest Cato,

This morning at four o'clock the Lord took our darling away from us. We had so much hoped for im-
provement, but this was not what God ordained. God
has strengthened us during all these events. We have
truly found that in Him there is grace and power. He is
a solid rock in all our need. I have nothing to say, since
I know for sure that He has allowed it. It was His will,
and His dealings are wise and loving, full of majesty
and glory. Knowing this gives me strength.

In another letter to Cato, Willem tells about his deep
inner struggles.

My dear Sister,

I am going through tremendous ups and downs. I do
so long to live in closer communion with the Lord of
eternity. But because of sin and unbelief, I miss that
light and life in my soul. Oh, my heart is so terribly
proud, such an enemy of all that is good! I must say
with Paul, I do not do the good I want, but the evil I do
not want is what I do.

Oh, my sister and friend, what a sad picture! However, I can say with John Newton (although not with as
much faith as he did), "My condition is painful but not
mortal. I will not die but live, for I have a gracious and
unfailing Physician."

Geertruide died. Two years later, Willem married
Elisabeth who had been the housekeeper for the bereaved
family for some time. She was young, energetic, and an
excellent housewife. This was helpful, for the frequent
illnesses had been a severe strain on the family budget, and
Willem's financial situation was precarious. Business was

not good. Willem had bought the house in the Barteljorisstraat in 1849 for 1200 guilders, and in addition, he had
to feed a large family.

Soon Elisabeth was expecting her first baby, and, in due
time, one could peer in through the scanty light in the bed-
room behind the watch shop and see a baby boy. Since
there was already a Willem among the sons of Grandfather's first marriage, this little boy was named Casper.

Now that his household was under the orderly manage-
ment of his young wife, Willem could look ahead with re-
newed courage and give himself to some of the activities in
the Kingdom of God that he loved. His letters to Cato became less depressed, often carrying a joyful note of vic-
tory.

Dear Cato,

Last week I was on an errand outside town, and had
to walk right across the sand dunes. Suddenly the sky
filled with black clouds; a terrible thunderstorm was
imminent. It thundered continuously. I took shelter in
a shack and looked about me. I saw a tree struck by
lightning. The violent wind broke many branches. I
stood there quietly, thunder and lightning all around
me.

All at once I was reminded of the majestic coming of
the Lord on the clouds of heaven. Oh, what glory I
saw! I thought of the day when I will see Him and cry
out, "My Redeemer, my Saviour!" Cato, then we will
be delivered from this body of sin. That day will come,
and every day brings us nearer to it.

In the middle of the nineteenth century, Holland was the
scene of a fresh revival movement that had a lasting effect
on the ten Boom family. In Heemstede, Nicolaas Beets

preached the Gospel under such anointing that many Haar-lemmers (among them the ten Booms) flocked to the nearby town to hear him.

The name *dauw trappers* was given to those members of Haarlem's population who sought spiritual refreshment in Heemstede. The words literally mean "those who go out into the country while the dew is still wet on the grass." The street that went from Haarlem to Heemstede in those days cannot be compared to the asphalt highway which is there now. Those who wanted to hear Nicolaas Beets had to walk through a lot of mud.

One of the fruits of the new spiritual awakening was the springing up of many organizations for the spreading of the Gospel and for the helping of those who were socially underprivileged. My grandfather became one of the founding board members of the Society for Christian Home Visitation and remained active in that capacity until his death.

Grandfather also became an elder of the Reformed Church of Haarlem. Being the first elected elder of orthodox conviction, he was in for a fierce battle. He courageously witnessed against rationalism, modernism, and unbelief, which were then characteristic of most of the formal churches in the Netherlands. He took a vital interest in the support of young people studying for the evangelistic or pastoral ministries, and spent much time visiting wealthy people to obtain contributions for these projects.

Prayers for Israel

In 1844, Willem started a weekly prayer meeting for Israel. It is not at all unusual for Christians to have prayer meetings for Jews in our modern times, but it was so unusual at that time that Father even remembered which year

Grandfather started his prayer group.

The Jews had found a refuge in Holland ever since the first Prince of Orange delivered our country from Spanish rule in the seventeenth century. Holland became a land of freedom and security for oppressed people from many countries. The Jews settled mainly in Amsterdam, and even called that city "the New Jerusalem."

We never know how God will answer our prayers, but we can expect that He will get us involved in His plan for the answer. If we are true intercessors, we must be ready to take part in God's work on behalf of the people for whom we pray.

One hundred years after Willem began his prayer meetings, his son, four grandchildren, and a great-grandchild were arrested in the same house where the prayer meetings started because they had saved Jewish people from Adolf Hitler's plans to kill them. Four of those arrested died in prison. That was the divine, but incomprehensible answer to my family's prayers for the Jewish people.

My nephew Peter and I found letters that told us more about the background of the prayer meetings for Israel. I found these sentences in one of Father's letters: "As long as I can remember, the portrait of Isaac Da Costa has been hanging in our living room. This man of God, with his burning heart for Israel, his own people, has had a strong influence on our family."

Isaac Da Costa, a Jew of Portuguese descent, was converted to Christianity and immediately set out to fight the spiritual forces that governed the Dutch people. He was a brilliant lawyer and a famous poet. As a result of the Enlightenment and the French Revolution, Europe had put reason above the Bible. Consequently, there was a general relaxing of godly standards in all levels of society.

Isaac da Costa with a bust of Nicolaas Beets: both of these men influenced the ten Boom family in their interest in spreading the Gospel to the Jews.

Immediately after his conversion, Da Costa wrote a book titled *Objections Against the Spirit of This Age.* The basic theme was taken from Scripture.

> For we are not fighting against people made of flesh and blood, but against persons without bodies—the evil rulers of the unseen world, those mighty satanic beings and great evil princes of darkness who rule this world; and against huge numbers of wicked spirits in the spirit world.
>
> Ephesians 6:12 LB

Immediately, a storm of protest and contempt broke loose upon the courageous young lawyer. He was mocked and scorned in the press.

A small circle of Hollanders stood with Da Costa. Among these was the ten Boom family. For these Christians, the clarion call of Da Costa meant the beginning of a new revival movement that left its mark on the whole spiritual atmosphere of nineteenth-century Holland. The Bible was restored to its place of authority as the Word of God.

In 1851 Da Costa attended the World Conference of the Evangelical Alliance in London. Two days were set aside there to discuss the work among Jews in the various countries represented. In the detailed report of this conference, I found an address by Da Costa which clearly states the reasons why he founded a number of prayer groups for Israel in various cities of the Netherlands. Here are a few thoughts from his interesting speech:

> Brethren, I see you are all rejoicing in the blessings of Christian fellowship. Even so, I have come here to ask for tears. Tears and prayers. Yes, I myself must

shed tears in your midst. For there is one nation which
has not been represented at this great international
gathering. It is God's own beloved people of Israel. Let
us remember that our Saviour, the Lord Jesus Christ,
who is now interceding for us at the Throne of God,
was born a Jew in a Jewish family in the nation of
Israel. It is true that Israel missed God's target and
was, for a time, set aside and dispersed among the
nations. But the day will come when they will fall at the
feet of their Messiah in true repentance and live! On
this occasion of the Great Exhibition, the Christians of
Great Britain have called the nations together on their
territory. The time will come when the King of the
Jews will call a holy gathering in Jerusalem. This is not
human imagination, but God's own Word through the
witness of another Jew, the Apostle Paul. He expresses
this expectation in Romans 11:15, "If their [Israel's]
rejection means the reconciliation of the world, what
will their acceptance mean but life from the dead?"
(RSV.)

We all agree that a strong bond ties us to Israel. As to
the past, Christianity is a fruit, an offshoot from the old
people of God. As to the present, is not Israel's existence among the nations, despite centuries of hostility
and persecution, one of the strongest proofs against the
world's unbelief? And as to the future, how clearly the
fulfillment of God's promises for Israel is related to the
future of the world and the coming Kingdom of Christ!
Well, then brethren! For these reasons I dare come to
you with an earnest plea. It is a custom in Israel at
certain great feasts, to keep an open seat for the
prophet Elijah. I request that you reserve an open seat
for Israel in our midst today. You lions of England and

Scotland, give full honour to the Lion from the tribe of Judah who has conquered! You, morning-watcher of the French people, announce the dawn of the day of His coming! You harp of Ireland, lead us in the song of expectation and longing of God's Church, "Come, Lord Jesus! Amen, come to bless and gather all the peoples of the world, also the long-rejected Israel in their midst! Amen."

Da Costa's work influenced my grandfather Willem to become one of the founders of the Society for Israel. Father often told us, "Love for the Jews was spoon-fed to me from my very youngest years." As a result, deep respect and love for the Jews became a part of our home life. How important childhood impressions are. Over the years, we often experienced the truth of God's promise to Abraham, "And I will bless them that bless thee . . ." (Genesis 12:3).

During the second half of the nineteenth century, the Jewish people slowly awakened to the need to return to their homeland. What had seemed an absolute impossibility for nineteen centuries—the establishment of a Jewish state in Israel, the land of the patriarchs—now became the vision of an Austrian reporter, Theodor Herzl. Herzl was not motivated by religious reasons; he thought only of survival for the Jews, but the return of the Jews to Zion was the beginning of the fulfillment of the Old Testament prophecies concerning Israel's restoration.

Is it presumptuous to think that the small prayer meeting in Haarlem was connected with these events? I believe that God delights to use His children in the fulfillment of His plans for the world. I am sure He loves to use small people to do great things. How honored I am to be part of His plan!

Willem ten Boom, Corrie's grandfather, was strongly interested in bringing the salvation message to the Jews. One hundred years after he began his prayer meeting for the Jews, Corrie and her family were taken by Adolf Hitler for hiding Jews in their home.

4
The Shape of Character

In his diary, Father writes about his parents, his childhood, and his teenage years spent in the little Beje. Before the Beje was enlarged, it did not afford much room for his large family. Father's childhood was not easy, but because of it, he learned to appreciate the good things in his life, and to find happiness in small blessings. Writing about his childhood, he tells:

A well-known psychologist once said, "When a child reaches his third birthday, his parents will have given him half of all that they will ever be able to give him in the way of education."

When I arrived on the scene, our small house in the Barteljorisstraat was already crowded. Father's first wife Geertruide, had died at the age of forty, leaving five children. I was the first child of the new marriage, and five more children were born after me.

Early in his second marriage, my father's business fared poorly, but my mother was a vigorous woman, with a strong will and lots of perseverance. She was an able seamstress and made all the underwear and linen clothes that were needed. I always wore clothes which had been handed down from my father or from one of my brothers, after Mother had altered them to fit me.

Mother was extremely economical and thrifty. Vegetables, meat, and other groceries were very inexpensive at that time, and she organized the household in such a way that living costs were kept to a bare minimum.

Sunday was the only day that we had a large and really tasty meal. During the week, the noon meal was often the same for weeks on end—rice, groats, brown beans, and an occasional small piece of bacon. On our birthdays, we would have a special meal.

My first memories go back to the time when I lay in the small crib which had been built squarely across my parents' bedstead, just above the foot of their bed. The bed was built inside a closet, the doors of which were left open while I was in my crib.

I remember how I would wake up on Sunday mornings and look at the shop from my crib. From my vantage point, I had a view of the living room and even the shop, when the doors that divided our living space from the shop were opened. During the week, the shutters of the shop window were closed, but on Sundays they were left open, and a blue striped curtain was lowered. How I enjoyed this special Sunday atmosphere.

On Saturday evenings, I was bathed and dressed in clean clothes. My mother always put a dash of brandy into the bath water. That particular smell and the fact that I received clean clothes made it all a real treat.

At the age of twelve, I became an apprentice in my father's watch-repair shop. He was a good-natured man, but a strict teacher. I am thankful that I learned punctuality from him. He was very exact, and required this from his apprentices and employees. When work-

ing, he was completely absorbed by what he was doing
and talked very little.

I never heard Father speak much about his own conversion. Once he told us about a man who was asked when he
had been saved. The man's answer was, "I was saved more
than nineteen centuries ago. It happened when the Lord
Jesus died on the cross for me and rose from the dead."

It is true that the ground of our salvation lies in Christ's
accomplished work, but Father knew about the need for a
personal acceptance of Jesus Christ as Saviour. From his
notebook, we have an account of his own spiritual experience.

I always went to church with my father. Pastor
Bronsveld came to Haarlem about 1870, and from my
earliest childhood, I enjoyed his sermons. Although
they did not provide great spiritual blessing for me, his
beautiful language and style, combined with great
simplicity, were a delight to me. Later I attended his
catechism class and became a member of his church,
where Father was an elder.

When I was confirmed at the age of eighteen, I had
already asked Jesus to come into my heart. I must have
been about seventeen when an evangelist named de
Ruiter came to spend a few days with us. He needed a
shave, and I took him to the barbershop belonging to
the father of one of my friends.

On the way, Brother de Ruiter suddenly turned to
me. "Casper, do you love the Lord?"

I answered him with a wholehearted "Yes." I believe that was the day of my conversion.

A short time afterward, I went to Ermelo for a vacation in the home of Pastor Witteveen. On Sunday morning there was a celebration of the Lord's Supper. I had a great desire to participate and told brother de Ruiter about it. He talked to the pastor, who had no objections as long as one condition was fulfilled. Before I could partake of the Lord's Supper, I had to make a public confession of my faith. I did this, and it was an important step for me. When I later made my confession in my home church, it was for the second time.

Now that I had found the Lord, or rather, He had found me, I was more interested in spiritual things than before. I spent many evenings talking to my friend Hartgerinck, who was a theological student at Amsterdam, where Da Costa was teaching. He shared with me what he learned from Da Costa. In this way, I received some theological training.

Father's Business

When my father, Casper, was eighteen years old, he went to Amsterdam to start a jewelry store in a poor section of the city. He had no money and no business experience, but did have a love for adventure and wide-open eyes for the people around him. The house where he started his business was small, so he found room and board with some Amsterdam people.

He lived in the Jewish section of Amsterdam, made contact with his neighbors very quickly, and was accepted by them to such an extent that he was even invited to join in their Jewish celebrations.

He joined a Christian young-men's group where he established lifetime friendships with several of the leaders. They started a work among poor people called *Tot Heil des*

Casper ten Boom as a young man. His faith was strongly influenced by his family, many of whom were active Christians.

Volks (For the Salvation of the People), and its headquarters are still in existence today, nearly a hundred years later. Father's great love for Amsterdam and the people of the city started at that time and never dwindled.

The organization contacted students at Amsterdam University, and these students started to help them in the *Tot Heil des Volks* work, inviting Father to work in their Sunday school. It was in that Sunday school that Father met Cor Luitingh, a teacher of one of the classes. He soon married her, and in 1884, the happy couple settled in the small house in Amsterdam.

Outwardly, the marriage was the beginning of years of trial for Father and Mother. They lived in a small watch

Corrie's mother with Betsie and Willem.

shop on a back street with few passersby. They had heavy debts, and suffered through Mother's poor health. Any one of these conditions can make for an unhappy home, but Father and Mother were close to each other, and they found that inner happiness does not depend on outward circumstances. Solomon was right when he said, "Better is little with the fear of the Lord than great treasure and trouble therewith" (Proverbs 15:16).

When the babies came one after the other, there were many reasons to worry. However, both Father and Mother increasingly enjoyed life, for they knew the art of living. Here are some lines from a letter which Father wrote to Mother when she was on a vacation in the country in 1887:

> What tremendous happiness we have in our children and in all of our family. The Lord is so good to us. It is my greatest joy to know that wherever we may be, you or I, the Lord looks down on us with favor and kindness, and that His Spirit lives in us.
>
> My dear wife, you are of such endless worth to me. I have no time to write more now. Enjoy the flowers and the plants, the singing of the birds, knowing they are a foretaste of heaven. Enjoy them, and as for me, do not worry at all. Fortunately, one more day of my solitude has come to its end.

And from another letter, written a year later by my father:

> I hope the Lord will bring days and years of prosperity to us. Still, we have nothing to complain about, for His loving kindness to us is immeasurable. My prayer for you, my dear wife, is that the Lord may

bless the medicine you take and complete your healing. How we shall thank Him if you prove to be healed. But whatever the outcome, we shall thank Him, because all His doings are pure love.

The important thing is that we live pure lives through His grace, that we grow purer, and that we come closer and closer to God. We must desire this with our whole hearts, for it is His will. I greatly long to have you home again and near to my heart, but if you need it, get more rest and stay until you are stronger. But you know how greatly I long for you. I kiss and embrace you with all my heart, and so do little Betsie and little Willem.

Mother kept a diary about her children. It was not strictly a diary, because sometimes she made only one entry a year, but what a precious book it was to us when she presented it to her children on her twenty-fifth wedding anniversary. It gave us such insight into her heart.

She wrote:

November 13, 1887

Our children are getting dearer every day. Three-year-old Betsie is a darling. She talks and sings the whole day long. It is so nice to hear her. I think she is very intelligent, because she learns so quickly and notices everything.

Our Willem is also a lovely child. He cannot walk yet, as Betsie did when she was a year old. This week he cut two teeth. He is happy and naughty in a very nice way. We cannot but thank the Lord for these lovely possessions; we enjoy them more and more.

Casper is such a proud father. It is a joy to see him with Betsie on his arm. He never complains when one of the children cries at night, and is always willing to help me.

Betsie fell down some stairs the other day. Casper heard her crying and ran from the workshop to comfort her in a way that never fails. He took her on his arm and showed her the pictures on the wall. He has an unlimited imagination in telling stories about what happened in the houses of a picture on the wall.

Father had to find another house. The Rapenburg, where he had his jewelry store, was a poor location, so he found a house close to the Queen's palace. Many more people passed this shop window, and he soon had more and better customers. Once a footman came from the palace with a clock that needed repair. What a privilege! When you worked in some way for the palace, you received a sign for your shop, stating *Hofleverancier* (by appointment to the court).

Father had then two workmen in his shop, a well-trained clockmaker and a teenaged apprentice. The royal clock had been repaired and was being packaged, when the boy who was holding it in his hands slipped, and the clock fell to the floor. Broken!

The boy looked at Father, who stood up, took a glass of water, and gave it to the white-faced boy. The boy was expecting a scolding or worse, but he heard Father say: "Boy, you have had a shock. Drink some water."

They were able to repair the clock, and something very special happened in the heart of that boy. He became Father's best watchmaker. Later, the boy became very ill. Father visited him regularly, and the boy died with his hand in Father's.

"I am going to Jesus," were his last words.

An Oak Tree in the Storm

Father was not always on top of his problems. Some of his letters tell of times when he was depressed and discouraged. Debts and financial difficulties often pressured him, and the house was often empty when Mother and some of the children went to the country to recover from their frequent illnesses.

He wrote:

June 4, 1889

My dear wife,

I do not want to make you wait any longer for news. Next Tuesday I have an appointment with Mr. H., who was recommended to me as somebody who might be able to help us. Once again I have hope that I will be delivered from these heavy burdens. I really feel like someone who is being tortured. I need to talk with somebody about my desperate financial situation. I can say without exaggeration that I have suffered deeply during these past few weeks.

However, there is a divine plan behind it all, and through suffering, we will get to glory. It has been the same way with you, my dear wife, and even though deliverance does not always come quickly, it does and will come. I know I am not always convinced of this truth, but I believe that God will show His faithfulness.

Wouldn't it be wonderful to be free of these burdens once again? The Lord will provide! I hope to receive some good news from you. Kiss and hug my dear Betsie and Willem and receive a warm embrace yourself from your loving husband.

Outwardly marriage was the beginning of years of trial for Corrie's parents. They found, however, that inner happiness did not depend on outward circumstances, but on the presence of Jesus in their hearts.

Mother wrote in her diary:

New Year's Eve, 1889

It is more than a year since I wrote in this book. I intended writing time and again, but I could not, and oh, it is still so hard to write about our beloved baby, our dear Hendrik Jan, whom we had received from the Lord on September 12, 1888 and whom we had to give back again on March 6, 1889.

It was such a joy to see how nicely Betsie and Willem treated him, how he smiled in response to them. What a grief it was to have to lose him. What a dreadful time it was, and our house is so empty. The Lord helped us through, and what a comforting thing it is that we already have a child in heaven, and that we will see him again.

It was touching to see how sad Betsie was. She missed him so much that she could not eat, and said over and over again, "The dear Lord must bring Hendrik back again."

They were both sitting next to Casper on the couch on Sunday afternoon and asked one question after the other.

"Does Hendrik see the dear Lord Jesus often?"

"Yes. Jesus loves him so much."

"Is Hendrik sometimes ill, like he was here?"

"No, nobody is ever ill in heaven."

"Will Hendrik be coming back soon?"

"No, Hendrik will not be coming back to us. We will go to him when the Lord Jesus takes us to heaven."

"When will He do that?"

"We don't know, but Jesus knows exactly when He is going to do it."

New Year's Eve, December 31, 1890

Another year has gone by. A really difficult year, full of cares and pain, and we moved house again. We are especially thankful to have been spared for another year, and that we are a dear little daughter richer in our Nollie. We are so very happy with her. She was such a great comfort and diversion in recent dark days. She is such a darling, with her blue eyes and dark hair, a really intelligent child, and I think she will be as quick as Betsie.

Father's Difficulty With Forgiveness

When Father saw the Germans during World War II put a group of Jews, including old people and children into police cars, he said, "Oh, that poor country! They have touched the apple of God's eye." Pity for Germany—love for his enemies. Was Father always like that? No.

It was difficult for Father to forgive. He had very high standards to live up to, and expected the same of other Christians. He could hardly bear it when Christians did things that were wrong but then acted piously.

When he was a young man starting his business in Amsterdam, Father did not know how to run a shop. A Christian man, a wholesaler in watches and clocks, gave him advice. Father trusted the man completely, and followed his advice, but the man deceived him. I do not know the details, for this happened before I was born, but I know that Father nearly went bankrupt several times because of the behavior of that so-called Christian.

Years later, when we passed this man's house, Father talked about the matter in an almost unforgiving way. Later, when the man experienced terrible difficulty with his family and his business, Father said it was because when a Christian behaves badly, he can expect immediate discipline.

I am so glad that God worked a miracle in Father's heart, so that through His love, Father could forgive. He needed that training when Germans, who said, "We have come to protect Holland," murdered members of his beloved family.

I remember walking with Father through Haarlem at that time. We saw swastika flags everywhere. I asked, "Father, are we allowed to hate a flag?"

He answered, "I believe we are, but not to hate the people. Hate the sins, love the sinners."

5

Return to the Beje

As his strength declined, my grandfather Willem became more and more occupied with the subject of death. The letters he wrote to Father had a serious tone, but they also expressed the joy in the hope of the coming deliverance. Here is a letter that he wrote a short time before his death. I especially like the practical afterthought.

Dear Casper,

I have some spare moments this morning, and want to write you a few lines. I notice from your last letter that you hope to receive strength for living and courage for dying. Let me tell you something: You do not need courage for dying yet. You will receive this only when you need it, not before, and you will receive it through the Lord Jesus Himself.

Death is not fiction; it is a great reality. The Lord Himself died, in order that death could become the road to heaven for us. He has taken away death's sting. Jesus lives in His church, and He supplies every member of His body with His power, just when it is needed. He will also do that at the time of one's death.

I think of Bunyan's story, where the Pilgrim has to go through the river of death and can feel no ground under his feet until somebody comes and lifts his head

50

out of the water. When we look at the body, we see it is only a travel outfit. The coffin and the dark grave show death in all its coldness, but we must look up to Him who is the conqueror of death.

The day when the saints enter into glory will be a great wedding for His church. Then we will be set free from all the bonds that hinder us from enjoying the love of Jesus and giving Him perfect praise. The Heidelberg Catechism, when treating the subject of death, rightly calls it "a passageway to eternal life." It is a cutting off of all sin, a dying to all that is vile and sinful. It means deliverance from the power of Satan, so that we will be eternally free to bathe in the love of God—no more darkness, no more strife.

As did the author and finisher of our faith, so we, as members of His body, need to go from Calvary to the Mount of Olives; through suffering to glory.

Therefore we can be of good courage, keeping a song of joy in our hearts and our eyes fixed on Him. The day of deliverance is coming, when we will sing with those who have gone on before us, "The Lamb that was slain is worthy to receive power, wisdom and honor, eternally, Amen" [*See* Revelation 5:12].

Many greetings from your father, Willem ten Boom. When I was with you last week, the front door was open and the children were sitting on the floor. You must not allow that. It is enough to make them ill, and it is not good for you, either. Your father.

On a cold December night in 1891, Father was called to the Beje, where his father lay dying. Grandfather approached death with quiet trust. In one of his last letters to his sister Cato, he wrote, "I am living one day at a time. God's goodness is eternal, and His faithfulness from generation to generation. I am so much enjoying the presence of the Lord, and I wait for Him. My suitcases are packed.''

With his last strength, Grandfather blessed Father with the apostolic benediction: "The grace of the Lord Jesus Christ, and the love of God, and the fellowship of the Holy Spirit, be with you. Amen.''

How my father needed that grace and love and fellowship when he was dying in a prison more than fifty years after this blessing from his father.

In the countries where I have worked, I find so many Christians who are afraid to die. It is true that death is the last enemy to be overcome, but it is still an enemy. However, does the Bible not show us clearly that our life here is not the last chapter of the book, but the first chapter?

> For we know that when this tent we live in now is taken down—when we die and leave these bodies—we will have wonderful new bodies in heaven, homes that will be ours forevermore, made for us by God himself, and not by human hands.
>
> 2 Corinthians 5:1 LB

From Amsterdam to Haarlem

Grandfather had often helped Father financially with the business in Amsterdam. When Grandfather's will was opened, Grandmother showed Father a list of all the money which Father had received. He had to pay it all back, which took him several years. A year later, Father was asked to come to Haarlem and work in Grandfather's shop with his mother. This was one of the hardest times in Father's life.

He rented a small house in Haarlem, and we lived away from the shop. When we moved, I was six months old, and Betsie was seven years old. Tante Anna, Mother's youngest sister, had always lived with us, so she was a member of our family, too.

Mother's diary tells of the changes our family went through during this period:

New Year's Eve, 1892

When I wrote in my diary exactly one year ago, none of us dreamed that this evening we should no longer be in Amsterdam. We left our beloved city in October, and are now living in a small, but nice, house in Haarlem.

There were so many changes! What an eventful year this was. At times it was so dark and difficult, but the Lord spared us for one another, and we also received a very small baby, which we had been expecting in May, but which arrived a month earlier, on Good Friday.

The Lord gave us a very little, weak baby—Corrie. Oh, what a poor little thing she was. Nearly dead, she looked bluish white, and I never saw anything so pitiful. Nobody thought she would live. And really, although she started to grow soon, she is still a weak child.

She is eight months old now, and is suffering from teeth that have not yet come through. I do hope they will be cut soon. None of the other children were so weak, and yet she is such a dear. She has very large eyes, and she looks so happy. She has to be treated very carefully. During the nights she is quiet, but in the daytime she can have terrible fits of crying. Her hair is dark, and she is a darling child when she is feeling quite well. I hope we may keep her.

Our Nollie is quite different. None of them looks as well as she does—so plump, and with good color. Her

dark eyes sometimes look nearly black, but they are
not as large as Corrie's eyes.

It is good to live here, because we can enjoy walking
in this part of the town so much more than in Amsterdam. Apart from that, there is a large garden behind
our house, from which we hope to have much pleasure
this summer.

A shadow on our living here is that we see so little of
Casper, as he is in the Barteljorisstraat all day and we
live in the Gaelstraat, a ten-minute walk away. Sundays are an even greater joy for us now. The children
are so happy then, because they can go for walks with
Daddy, who tells them stories.

New Year's Eve, 1895

Our children are growing up. Betsie is as good as
ever and developing nicely. She is learning well and
doing her best always. She does everything at her own
speed, and that can be rather slow, but oh, she is such a
dear, warmhearted daughter to us.

Our Willem has changed a lot in his favor this past
year. The reason was a very nice one. During the
summer, the Salvation Army held open-air meetings
every Sunday in our part of town, and Betsie and Willem attended them regularly. Willem soon told us that
he wanted to become a young soldier, and when we
explained to him that he had to show this by fighting
against all his faults, he said, "Well, I am going to do
so." And it was a miracle how he gradually changed
and persevered, even in the smallest things. May the
Lord bless his endeavors.

Nollie grew thin and pale this year. She loves learning, and is teaching herself to read and write. We can
see in many ways that she is very intelligent.

Our Corrie is still the youngest, and is so sweet. Everyone is fond of her. She is much more childlike than the others were at that age, but she has such lovely manners. We have to take special care of her. She has frightened us so often, especially by shouting wildly in her sleep. She has to be kept very quiet.

So there are nothing but blessings with our children. But on the other hand, some very dark clouds have come up, and it is impossible to write it all down. It concerns my husband and his mother. That problem has been going on for such a long time. What a terrible thought, that a mother is not living in peace with her own children. So many prayers have been offered for this very sad state of affairs. I only trust that the difficulties will not grow too severe for my dear Casper. He looks so unwell. May the Lord cause it all to end well.

Grandmother left the shop and the house a few years later, making it possible for us all to live in the same house as the business. However, it was necessary to enlarge and remodel the Beje. Father and a friend, an architect, drew up the plans for the reconstruction of the Beje, planning five small rooms on the third floor of the building. When the Beje became a refuge for so many Jewish people years later, it was very practical to have so many tiny rooms.

Business was going better for Father.

The Beje

Mother wrote:

New Year's Eve, 1897

We had to put off the renovation of our house altogether, and then the Lord brought it about in a very

special way. Men are working on it now, and they hope
to have it ready within a few months. Both grownups
and children are so looking forward to its being
ready—especially me. It is being enlarged, and will be
very practical. Casper is enjoying the work very much.
It is lovely when an ugly and unattractive object is
turned into something so good. What a change for the
family.

It was just a house, but I lived there for more than fifty
years. It was still an impractical house—with steep, narrow, winding stairs—far too small for ten people to live in.
On the right and left were much taller houses, so little sun-
light reached our windows.

When I came back from prison, I met a cousin who had
moved into the Beje after his house was confiscated.
"What a dark house this is," he said. "We need electric
lights on in the living room and workshop almost all day." I
had never once realized that. To me, the Beje was light!

The Beje was Father, Mother, and around them,
people—young and old—who lived intensely and whose
horizons were so much wider than the walls of this pecu-
liarly built little house. Its door may have been narrow, but
it was always wide open to every person who needed help.

Privileged

The very first generator to produce electric light in our
town was placed in the block of houses where we lived. The
noise of the motor could be heard day and night, but ours
were the only houses in Haarlem which had the privilege of
possessing electric light switches.

During prayer, Mother always turned the light off—why
use electricity when everybody had their eyes closed? But

one day, during prayer, the doorbell rang. Everybody in the room ran to the light switch at once, causing many collisions in the pitch dark. That was the most hilarious prayer time ever held in the Beje!

Tante Jans said afterwards, "In spite of this, I hope that we will put off the lights again during our prayers."

The generator would break down often in those days, at which time all of us living in that block of houses would hear a familiar *bang*. The lights would be off for days, sometimes for weeks, until the motor was finally repaired. This usually happened when we had a large crowd of visitors, a board meeting, or something else that made the mishap nothing less than a catastrophe. The motor in our block caused us to praise the Lord often, but it also gave us many laughs together.

The Radio

In a Bible class one day, a servant girl told us that her employer shared the ownership of a new invention—radio—with several other people on his block.

"Every month we have the radio in our home for one day," she told us. "It is a small box, and it gives music and speaks. There is a big thing on top that looks like a horn."

"Do you have something like wires in your ears to hear it?" we asked.

"No. We all sit around and we hear singing and speaking as if it were happening in the very room."

"Can you hear several voices at once?"

"Yes. Sometimes we hear a whole orchestra!"

Some time after I shared the story of the radio at home, the children of Haarlem gave Father a radio. How excited we were when it had been installed and we could try it out! We gathered near the radio expectantly, and the first thing we heard from it was the song, "My Bonny Lies Over the Ocean."

How we laughed—that was the one song that Betsie could not stand!

Betsie was put in charge of selecting the radio programs we would all listen to. She would carefully read the weekly program listings, then mark every interesting program with a red pencil. Thanks to Betsie, we never missed one worthwhile program on this fantastic new invention.

There was no electricity at all in Holland during the last years of the German occupation. Shortly after the war, I went to America. Imagine how I felt when I saw the many colored streetlights in New York, and lighted windows in empty rooms. During that time, I would often turn off the lights in empty rooms without thinking. When I told my hostesses the story of the privileged Haarlem people, they always understood and forgave me.

Blessing

Two shadows brought darkness into our lives—the chronic money shortage and Mother's frequent illness. I remember often asking my father, "Why, Papa. Why?" I found his answer in a story in his notebook.

It happened around the year 1640. A group of Spaniards was traveling through the jungles of South America when one member of the party fell seriously ill with malaria. In a short time, the fever weakened him so much that he was unable to walk.

His friends were at their wits' end. They improvised a stretcher from branches and tried to carry him on it. The condition of the sick man and the difficulties in transporting him became such that they finally decided to lay him down at the side of a pool of water, in the shadow of a tree with thick foliage. There they left him.

His situation seemed desperate. His fellow travelers had left him some food, but he paid no attention to it. *Water!* That was his only thought. Tormented by a burning thirst, he bent down to the water, only to fall back in despair. The water had a loathsome and bitter taste.

But as time went on, and the fever continued to burn and consume his body, he drank again and again. Then a strange thing happened. After every drink of water, the fever seemed to subside and the pain to become less severe. Strength returned to his weak body.

Healing had come to him through the bitterness of the water. You see, the tree under which his companions had laid him was the Cinchona, or quinine tree. Leaves and pieces of bark had fallen into the water, and the quinine had dissolved. Not only was the exhausted traveler completely restored, but a wonderful remedy was discovered, through which countless lives have since been saved.

That is the way it often goes with those of us who have to pass through dark and bitter trials. How easily we rebel against the circumstances that cause us to suffer and which we cannot change. However, the Lord sends troubles our way in order to heal us. We must believe in His love and wisdom. Soon we discover that the bitterness of the medicine was necessary in order to heal us.

Watchmaker by the Grace of God

"My name is on the shop," my father often said, "but God's name should really be there. I am a watchmaker by the grace of God."

Can God help us solve practical, everyday problems? In 1899, Father wrote to his Aunt Cato:

At present I am using my spare time to study the regulating of precision watches. In fact, I have been doing so for quite some time, and I am getting many blessings out of it.

Some weeks ago, I was occupied with a difficult technical problem in my work. I studied several books on the subject, which were, as is all watchmaking literature, in English and German. I searched many books, but could not locate the necessary information.

Then, one night in a dream, I saw a drawing of white lines and dots on a black background, with an explanation beside it in English and German. It was so simple and clear that I understood it at once.

The next morning I tried it, and it worked! The problem was solved perfectly. Once again, I reviewed all my books to see if I could find a drawing like the one I had seen in my dream, but I found none. I can say that, even in such worldly matters, the Lord is my Shepherd. Such experiences enable me to persevere in the difficulties in my business, for I am certain that the Lord is with me and helps me.

Impossible to Repair

Father liked the challenges of watches or clocks which were declared impossible to repair. Once we read, in the paper of the Salvation Army, a story by the wife of a Salvation Army officer, Mrs. Celestine Oliphant-Schoch. She traveled all over the world with her family, and every time she packed her belongings for another move, the last item she would pack was an old clock that played the song "What a Friend We Have in Jesus."

When they arrived at a new post, that clock would be the first thing she would unpack. Listening to its tune, she would immediately feel at home, no matter where she was in the world.

The woman who wrote the story was retired and living in Switzerland. At the end of her article, she mentioned that her clock was broken, apparently beyond repair.

After reading the story, Father went to the Salvation Army headquarters in Haarlem and asked that the clock be brought to him the next time someone came from Switzerland to Holland. He was able to repair the clock, and we soon heard the song ringing from our workshop. It gave Father great pleasure to be able to ship the clock back to the lady from the Salvation Army, in perfect working order.

The ten Boom children were often a part of their parents' letters, when they were away. The love of their parents was obvious in the letters Corrie found. From left to right, the children are: Betsie (seated), Corrie (standing), Nollie, and Willem.

as an officer in Jesus' army, fighting on the front lines, involved—locally, nationally, and also internationally—in as many opportunities as came his way. In fact, my father lived on a more international level than most people of his time, for he regularly studied books and magazines printed in four different languages.

Father made his most important international contacts through the *Union Horlogere,* a watchmakers' organization in which many European nations were represented. Once a year he went to Switzerland for the organization's annual meeting. Besides the business meetings, there was always a banquet, and Father was one of the best speakers there.

Here, he again saw people who were neglected. The del-

you to me. It may sound strange, but I think it is a proof of His great goodness that although He sustains me through so many difficulties, at the same time He causes me to be so thoroughly happy with you and our children. Perhaps the flame of my love may not burn as strongly as in the beginning. However, I can say that I have not abandoned my first love for you. It has never lessened. May the Lord grant that both of us may increase in love for each other and for Him.

We children were confident of our parents' interest in all our experiences, and by their example, they encouraged our interest in other people. After an unexpected treat, when good friends had visited us, when we had sung and made music together, Father would often remark, "Children, the greatest joy for us all is that these happy hours were just a little foretaste of the joys which we will experience in heaven. The best is yet to be."

My parents loved company, music, good literature. They had the gift of being able to enjoy each other, the children, and the many other things that were important in their eyes.

Life was different then, very different from now. Because of air travel, television, international life-styles, we now live much more complicated lives. We are world citizens. Our bodies, souls, and minds are caught up, not just in our own problems, but in the concerns of an entire world. We must endure and suffer pollution, chaos, the challenge of money or the lack of it, financial breezes and storms, crime and terrorism—not only in our own countries—but all over the world. We cannot be indifferent to what happens in China, Belfast, and Uganda. We are hurt and threatened by what happens there when things go wrong.

Whenever I think of what I saw of Father's life, I see him

Father and Mother belonged together. Father was the strong man who sustained Mother, who was weak in health, but strong in character. They worked as a team. As a couple, they shared deeply. Mother never complained, not even when needy persons were taken in at a time when the smallest expenditure had to be weighed carefully. Her body was weak, and yet she was full of energy. When she could no longer walk, she made a garden on the flat roof of the Beje and pulled herself around to tend her beloved plants.

Father and Mother lived life to the fullest. They understood the art of living, and that gave them greatly enlarged horizons. Though the quantity of material things was extremely limited, the quality of life was great. Neither was afraid to get involved when people were in need. They shared their home, their food, their money, and their God. This kind of love relationship can stand the wear and tear of years of trials and troubles. After eight years of happily married life, Father wrote this to Mother, who was visiting friends in another place:

Don't think that I have forgotten you, even though I have not written for three days. On the contrary, I become more and more convinced that the Lord granted me an overwhelming privilege when He gave

6

Father and Others

The ten Boom family with the first grandchild. From left to right: Tine, Baby Casper, Willem, Nollie, Corrie, Mother, Betsie, and Father.

1916–1920. Their first babies were born there.

Tine fitted into the role of pastor's wife very well. She was a source of constant encouragement and moral support to Willem, who found it difficult to minister among the rural population. The good, solid, and sometimes stubborn Dutch farmers by no means accepted all that Willem preached, although he tried to express his spiritual experience in terms that they would understand.

Willem was very fortunate in having a wife who possessed what he did not have—a special gift of expression. The many beautiful poems she wrote are a lasting testimony. Tine used to say, "My husband digs the gold—I beat it into coins." Her prayer life was also a vital factor in Willem's ministry. He wrote to the Beje:

> The scope of my ministry seems to be diminishing, and we are getting more and more depressed. Yes, but also, the Lord sustains and helps us more and more. I am very weary of preaching without response. During this past week, the Sunday morning service loomed before us like a high mountain. But this morning, Tine stayed home and spent the whole time in prayer for me. The church was fuller than I had expected, and the Lord surprised me by granting me unusual support and greater boldness.

Willem lacked the practical insight necessary to solve the many small problems of a village parish. He soon came to grips with the matter of education and urged the creation of a Christian school. In this, he seemed to come into conflict with some of the rich and influential church members. When he refused to compromise, persecution and hostility set in.

Many a desperate call for prayer found its way from Wil-

egates from Czechoslovakia understood a little German, but nobody knew their language. How happy they were when Father, who gave a short talk in six languages, also gave a seventh talk—in Czech. He had asked the help of one of the teachers at the Berlitz school, who had written his Czech message out phonetically for Father.

Still, the most important outlet for his wisdom, his love, and his daily attention was his hometown of Haarlem, including the local organizations with which he worked. He became a member of the Rehabilitation Association, which took care of ex-prisoners and their families, and was elected chairman of the board after only a few weeks' service. That happened with many of the boards of which he became a member. He had an intense interest in every human being he met. He was loving, gifted, and hard working.

Whether he was in the Chamber of Commerce, the local school, or any other place where he was on the board , if he saw somebody being persecuted, ill-treated, or wrongly criticized, he rose to his defense. Everybody who was oppressed could count on his help.

When the Nazis occupied Holland and forced the Jews to wear the yellow Star of David so they could be quickly singled out for punishment or imprisonment, it is not surprising that Father reported in the line to get his Star of David. It was the only way, at the moment, for an old man to protest the oppression of his brothers. His international citizenship was never more obvious than then.

Once Father was hospitalized for a severe illness. Each day, our local newspaper reported on his condition, until he was able to go home. Dutch people love to take walks, and Father was eager to get out for a stroll again. His first walk after his recovery still stands out in my mind.

What a lot of hands he had to shake—little hands, big

Corrie's father was much loved in Haarlem. He was affection-
ately known as "Haarlem's grand old gentleman."

hands, hands calloused from hard labor, and well-manicured, soft hands. A car came to stop beside us, and the mayor of Haarlem stepped out to greet Father, saying, "Thank God that you are better!" Grown men stood with tears of joy in their eyes as they greeted him. "Haarlem's grand old gentleman" was back again!

What was the source of his sensitivity toward people, which caused him to be so unashamedly loved by the people of his community? The cornerstone of his character was his steady and consistent walk with the Lord, his knowledge of, and trust in, the Bible. He believed the Bible was relevant for every part of his daily life. He started each day in the workshop with a word of prayer and a Scripture reading with all his family and workers.

When he met anyone interested in the Bible, he did not hesitate to invite him or her to his Bible-study groups. He once told us about the extraordinary combination in his group studying the Book of Romans. There were agnostics, atheists, fundamentalists, a Calvinist, a liberal, and a Roman Catholic.

Sitting behind his workbench in the shop, Father was an ambassador for Christ, a representative of heaven. His everyday life was to the honor of the Lord. People who came into the shop often stopped to watch Father work. They would walk into the workshop, lean against the table, and watch how he carefully cleaned the watch he had undertaken to repair.

Dutch prime minister Abraham Kuiper's daughter, a gifted young woman who wrote articles for magazines, often came and stood there, talking with Father or just watching his skillful hands. He was always ready to listen. He was always concerned for people.

The eminent Professor Lorenz lived in our town, and he

Casper ten Boom became an apprentice in his father's watch-repair shop. He began his own shop at age eighteen and later became respected in international watchmaking circles.

sometimes came to discuss his latest discoveries in chemistry with Father. I could not follow their conversations, but once he asked about the radium which we put on the watches to make them visible in the dark. Because Father read magazines in so many languages, he had learned about this latest discovery earlier than his colleagues. He gave a few samples to Professor Lorenz. "It is a privilege that God gave me this opportunity to do something for such an important man," Father said later to me.

Sundays were the happiest days of the week. Everyone knew that a Christian did not work on Sundays. Not even needlework was allowed. The one labor still permitted was the winding of the watches that had been repaired and were being regulated. Father always said, "I must milk my cows." However, he did not do the work in the shop, but brought the watches into our living room. In my mind, I still see his freshly brushed black suit, long, neatly trimmed beard, white hair, and sparkling eyes. As he carefully wound each watch, he would sing Psalm 84, "Blessed is the man whose strength is in thee . . . ."

Hospitality in the Beje

Once when Tante Anna was in the hospital, she found that Alida, her roommate, had no home. She had a live-in job, but she never had a place to spend her days off, so the Beje became her home.

I remember that she was used to crying very often. She was moved to tears when she was happy and when she was unhappy. I fear that I was not too patient with her, since every time I hurt myself when I was a child, Father would say, "Grit your teeth. Be a big girl and don't cry."

Mother did not agree. "Cas, let her cry. It relieves the nerves," she would say.

Alida once confessed, "Before I go to the Beje, I always cry a little bit in my room, because I know it is not allowed at the Beje."

Father was always interested in the people who came to us, and in his prayers after the meal, he laid before his heavenly Father all the problems which were in the lives and hearts of our guests. Once, when I started to make the bed of one of the guests, I saw that one of the sheets had been crumpled and twisted into the shape of a rope. I asked Tante Anna what had happened, and she went to our guest and asked her to explain.

"I am so ashamed to tell you," was her reply. "I was intending to hang myself with that sheet, but just as I was going to do it, I remembered Casper's prayer after the meal, and I stopped."

Tante Cato's Birthday Party

When I was young, Tante Cato, Grandfather's sister, was still alive. She was Father's favorite aunt and became a legendary figure for us children. Year after year, Father took us to Amsterdam to visit her on her birthday. These pilgrimages were special events.

Tante Cato was a very special lady, with lively dark eyes. She ran a large kindergarten in Amsterdam, and that was always our first stop during our annual visits. Tante Cato greeted us delightedly, showed us through the school, and then we joined in the great celebration that the children of the kindergarten had planned.

The last time I can remember, each child wore a soldier's cap and carried a little wooden sword. Tante Cato wore a cap and beat vigorously on a drum hanging around her waist. I can still see her, an eighty-year-old woman, heading up the parade. She marched proudly around the big room with all the children behind her, singing loudly.

I remember thinking, "I hope that when I am eighty, I will be so fit and healthy that I will have as much fun as she is having with these children."

In the evening there was a little dinner which followed the same pattern every year. The dessert was followed by Father's birthday speech. He took his Bible from his pocket, read Psalm 103 and gave a well-prepared little talk. The reaction of Mina, the maid, who was also not so young, was the same every year. She wore the old-fashioned maid's uniform—a dark blue dress with a long white apron. She was moved to tears every year and dried her eyes with the corner of her apron. Tante Cato did not shed tears, but how happy she was to listen to what Father said about the Lord whom she loved with her whole heart.

The Watchmaker-Counselor

Many people sought advice from Father. The stability of his faith and his good common sense made him an excellent counselor. His judgment was never hasty. He took time to pray about the matter and think things over. Those who received help remember his rare ability to encourage and stimulate the good in others—a quality so necessary in counseling.

Tante Jans' husband, Hendrik Wildeboer, once had to make a decision concerning which of two towns he should serve as a pastor. He chose the tiny town of Oudewater over a bigger town with more possibilities. After his decision, Father wrote him this letter:

September 15, 1887

Dear Hendrik,

No pen can describe how delighted I am that you have accepted the call to the pastorate in Oudewater. When I last wrote I did not want to dissuade you in any way from going to IJmuiden, because I felt you had to make your choice yourself, alone, without any influence from those who love you. Now we thank the Lord from the bottom of our hearts that you had the courage to do His will. Whatever the sacrifice is, the Lord will make it up to you. He has more to give you than this.

I could not help thinking of the choice Lot made when he chose the fertile plains of Sodom. Your decision may seem a stupid move to many, for those in the world, and out for advantage, will rarely choose the Saviour's way. You have acted as a man, as a prince, as one who aims straight at the goal.

". . . he that believeth shall not make haste" (Isaiah 28:16). Just wait your time. You do not need to

Here is a painting by Bernard de Hoog, showing Corrie's Uncle
Hendrik, Tante Jans's husband, preaching.

be afraid of anything. Who knows what God has in
store for you?

(Hendrik Wildeboer became, later, pastor in the big town
Rotterdam.)

On one of our morning walks, Father and I passed the
bookstore of Mr. Vernhout. He was a small man, with lively
eyes and a little pointed beard. Mr. Vernhout was standing
at the open door, and when he saw Father, he asked if he
could step inside for a moment. In the little office
behind the store, the old man told Father his problem.

The owner of the house and store had to sell the property,
and had offered it to Mr. Vernhout, who rented it from him.
However, the purchase would mean an enormous drain on
the small business. Father suggested that they pray about it,

and both knelt down on the office floor. It was an impressive sight: two dignified, bearded men, humbly bowing before their God.

When they rose, Father said, "I am convinced that you should buy the house." Mr. Vernhout did so, and the following years confirmed that it was the right decision. The bookstore is still there today and is a flourishing business. Whenever I pass it, I think of how important it is to acknowledge God in all our ways, including our business decisions.

Father always used the Bible when he counseled. He knew that the needs of people are not sufficiently met by human philosophies. He always knew a Bible verse that precisely answered the need of those who came to him. I asked him once, "Papa, do you learn by heart every text that you think will be useful for counseling people?"

"No," he answered, "it is the Lord who gives me the words I need." He mentioned Isaiah 50:4:

The Lord God hath given me the tongue of the learned, that I should know how to speak a word in season to him that is weary . . . .

"The Lord desires, far more than I, to help these people, and He uses you and me. But, girl, don't forget that every word you know by heart is a precious tool that He can use through you."

I have often thought about those words. During the freezing cold hours of roll call in the concentration camp, the Holy Spirit would bring verses to my mind that I did not remember having learned. I would then use them at the Bible lesson later in the day. How precious it is when we have God's Word hidden deep in the corners of our hearts.

7
Throwing Out the Lifeline

Father gave his evangelistic messages careful preparation. The following story was part of a message on Isaiah 55:1: ". . . every one that thirsteth, come ye to the waters, and he that hath no money; come ye, buy, and eat; yea, come, buy wine and milk without money and without price."

An artist once wanted to paint a ragged, miserable beggar. No matter how hard he searched, it seemed impossible to find a beggar who looked pitiful enough to serve as a model.

One day, crossing a square in town, he noticed an old man clothed in rags sleeping on a wagon. What a heap of human misery! This was his man!

Shaking him out of his sleep, the artist said, "My friend, would you like to earn a guilder a day?"

You can understand that the poor man accepted the offer with both hands.

"Well," said the artist, "come to my home tomorrow morning at ten o'clock. Come just as you are, with exactly the same clothes on."

The next morning, at the appointed hour, the doorbell rang at the painter's house. As he opened the door, he saw that the beggar had mended the holes in his clothes and shined his shoes. His face and hands were

78

clean, and his hair neatly combed. He looked like a different man.

The artist shook his head. "No, my friend, I have no use for you this way. I chose you because you were poor and miserable. I need you just as you looked yesterday—as you really are in everyday life. I am sorry, but I cannot use you."

The Lord Jesus calls you to come to Him just as you are. He desires with all His heart to give you His riches; you do not need to bring anything. Yes, for the very reason that you have nothing, He will give you everything. Jesus said, "For the Son of man is come to save that which was lost" [Matthew 18:11].

In later years, Father wrote to my brother Willem:

You must be careful to control your feelings and not repeat the same thought, even when you do it with somewhat different words. A sermon must be a journey in thought with a definite aim, preferably a climax. You are like a guide who leads a company of travelers up a mountain, to a point where their vision is clear and far. So, in preaching, do not dwell on points which you have already passed.

Father understood the mentality of the people of his time. During the last half of the nineteenth century, there had been an overemphasis on man's personal experience. People thought they needed to feel deep sorrow and shed tears over their sinfulness before they could obtain forgiveness. Many would try to analyze their own feelings and were afraid that their conviction of sin was not strong enough. This dependence on one's own feelings caused young believers to fall into doubt and despair. Father understood these dangers.

When Jesus calls you, sinners, come! What is hindering you? I know. You are saying, "Not yet, because I do not feel sufficiently that I am a sinner. It is only when I have really felt the heaviness and thirst of my soul that I can come to the source. Before that, I cannot be saved."

No, fellow, this is not necessary. Jesus never said this. All He wants from you is that you simply believe—and only believe.

"But," you may ask, "how far must I go? How long does it last until I can obtain it?"

It is so near. It cannot be nearer. The fish cannot get any nearer to the water, and the bird cannot get any closer to the air. You cannot get any closer to Jesus. His love is surrounding you on all sides. Through His finished work on the cross, He can save you from all your sins—right now.

I found in Father's notebook the following stories that he used in his talks.

Father is Holding the Rope

A traveler in Armenia crossed the country in search of rare plants and flowers. On one of his trips he noticed, in a deep cleft of a rock, a flower of such rarity and beauty that he decided to pick it, whatever it might cost him.

But how could he do it? The sides of the rocks were so steep that it was impossible to climb down to where

the flower was. The only way would be to let someone
down into the crevice on a rope. But who would risk
his life to do that?

After some searching, he found a boy and asked him
to go down and pick the flower for a good sum of
money. He encouraged the boy by saying, "I will hold
the rope very firmly."

But the boy shook his head. "I would not do that for
all the money in the world! However, if my *father*
comes to hold the rope, I will do it."

The child of God is often in danger, hovering over
precipices, but he can be joyful and calm, because his
heavenly Father is holding the rope, and he is safe. In
Psalms 94:18, David said, "When I said, My foot slipp-
eth; thy mercy, O Lord, held me up."

This story of Father's reminds me of the words of Oswald
Chambers, whose book of daily meditations, *My Utmost
for His Highest,* was used by my parents in our prayer
times.

The nature of spiritual life is that we are certain *in*
our uncertainty. We are uncertain of the next step, but
we are certain of God. Spiritual life is the life of a child.
We are not uncertain of God, but uncertain of what He
is going to do next. A joyful uncertainty and expec-
tancy . . . .

Daddy Knows

"Where are you going, little lady?" asked the driver
of the double-decker bus in London.

The only person in that part of the bus was a very

little girl, who was sitting quietly in the corner. At first she did not answer, but after a moment's hesitation she said, "I'm going home."

The driver whistled a little tune, then asked again, "But where are you *really* going?"

"Home," was the answer, this time in a rather worried tone.

"But where do you get out?"

The child looked at him with a puzzled expression, but suddenly her face lit up and she said happily, "I don't know, but my Daddy knows." Then she pointed to the ceiling. "He is upstairs."

Indeed, at the following stop, a broad-shouldered man came down the stairs from the upper deck and called, "Come on, Rosy. This is our stop."

Isn't it good that we can say, as that little girl did, "Father knows." Whatever may happen, let us remember and say, "Father knows. He is upstairs."

As David said in Psalm 40:17, "I am poor and needy; yet the Lord thinketh upon me . . . ."

My Child Is Drowning

Some time ago, I was in London. During my trip, I had to cross the great London Bridge. On one side of the bridge, I noticed a number of people crowding along the waterfront and looking down into the water. I asked someone what had happened.

"There is a child in the water," was the answer. Then from left and right, I heard people calling out, "A child is drowning!"

Suddenly a shrill voice was heard that struck everyone with terror. *"My child* is in the water!"

It was clear to all that there is a vast difference between the statement "A child is in the water" and the personal cry from the mother's heart, *"My child* is drowning."

Not only that, God gave His Son in order to save us, and this did not leave Him indifferent. For Him you are not *a* child, but *my* child. What does that tell you about God's great love for you? What a tremendous price He paid to bring us out of sin to Himself.

The Bible says it in Romans 8:32. "He that spared not his own Son, but delivered him up for us all, how shall he not with him also freely give us all things?"

Father as an Ambassador

Besides preaching himself, Father helped and encouraged others to do so. He was vitally interested in anybody who made the Lord Jesus known as the crucified and risen Saviour. I found a letter which he wrote to Mother in 1889, when they were still living in Amsterdam.

Last night Anna and I were walking in the street and noticed a crowd gathering along one of the canals. As we got near, we saw that the subject of their curiosity was a man on crutches, who appeared to be a worker of the Midnight Mission [a work which tries to reach the prostitutes].

We started to chat with him. Meanwhile, the prostitutes who were standing close by began to curse and scream in a terrible way. When they saw that we were standing with the missionary, they, of course, began to insult us, too. We were honored, and in no small measure.

Father was in excellent company. It was said of our Lord Jesus that He was a friend of winebibbers and sinners. Many years later, when I started Gospel work among the mentally retarded people of Haarlem, Father encouraged me. "Corrie, every single person is so important in God's eyes. In the eyes of God it could be that what you are doing now is the most important work in the whole world!"

Father's Attitude When Serious Things Happened

Once Mother came into the workshop and said, "Cas, the *Titanic* has sunk. We heard about it over the radio."

Father went to the living room with Mother and called everybody who was at home. We had all heard about the big ship—it was so safe, so luxurious.

Father did not accept the news and put it aside. I remember how he talked it over, even with the customers. There was a little antique drawing in the shop, of an old-fashioned clock shop, with the words, *Dat men bereid is Terwyl het tyd is* (One has to be ready for when the time comes).

"Just think," Father said. "The passengers on the *Titanic* did not think much about danger. Those who belonged to the Lord Jesus were ready. Perhaps God called some at the last minute. The ship's orchestra band played 'Nearer My God to Thee' until the moment that they drowned."

Use the acceptable time. Just ask yourself—now that there is still time, am I ready to face a righteous God?

De HOROLOGIEMAAKER.

Dat men bereid is Terwyl het tyd is.

ô Mens, befchik uw zielenftaat,
Terwyl des levens uurwerk gaat;
Want als 't gewigt is afgeloopen
Van deezen korten leevenstyd,
Daar is geen ophaal weêr te koopen,
Voor konft, noch geld, noch achtbaarheid.
Ro-

This is a copy of an engraving that hung in Casper ten Boom's shop. The Dutch is translated: People's Trades/The Watchmaker/One has to be prepared for when the time is over./O man arrange your state of soul/As long as the clock is still going;/For when the weight has come to the end/Of this short time that we live,/You can't pay anybody anywhere to pull the weight up again,/Not through art, or money, or respect of man.

8
Father and His Son

Psalm 128:1–3 sings of the joy of the man who fears the Lord and walks in His ways. His wife is compared to a fruitful vine within his house, his children, to olive shoots around his table.

One of the olive shoots which grew up around the oval table at the Beje was Willem, the only surviving boy of the ten Boom children.

Praise and Prison

Let us go back to the year 1892. Tante Jans was sitting in a circle with her girls' club. A frail five-year-old boy was sitting next to her. He had large, dark eyes. This was a birthday party for one of Tante Jans' club girls, and little Willem was allowed to attend.

After the lemonade and cookies, Tante Jans took her Bible, and following the old tradition for every birthday, read Psalm 103. "Bless the Lord, O my soul . . . bless his holy name . . . and forget not all his benefits . . . ." She then suggested that the girls mention some of the things for which they could praise God.

"That none of us has died," said one.

"That we are all in good health," added another.

Suddenly the little boy pulled his aunt's sleeve and, with

a grave look in his dark eyes, said, "Tante Jans—that we have not been put in prison!"

Little Willem did not know that one day, more than half a century later, he would be put into prison—and that he would be able to thank God for even that.

Too Many Guardian Angels

There were no serious problems in Willem's youth, although he might have suffered a little from the overwhelming majority of women in the house. Besides his mother and three sisters, there were the three aunts, all doing their part to see that he grew up to be a good boy.

But, in spite of this overdose of the feminine touch, his youth was very happy. There is no evidence of any real clashes between him and his father. On the contrary, there seems to have been a beautiful, harmonious relationship between them.

However, I do remember one incident. When Willem was fifteen years old, he began to attend the *Wapenhandel* on Saturday afternoons. This was the training which teenagers received to prepare them for service in the army. Whenever Willem started anything, he did it with his whole heart. He very much liked playing soldier!

Once, during examination time, Willem needed to prepare for a Monday examination. Since he was not allowed to study on Sunday, Father told him not to go to the *Wapenhandel* on Saturday, but to prepare for Monday's test, instead. I looked at Willem's face and saw that he was making the decision not to obey Father.

Suddenly, at mealtime, Willem jumped up, ran to the door and out into the street. Without hesitating, Father ran after him, and, in the middle of the street, took hold of Willem's shoulder in a strong grip and brought the captive

boy back into the house. I remember hearing Willem running upstairs to his room. It was a conflict the like of which
had never happened before, and I started to cry.

Years later, when Willem was no longer a boy, he said,
"That strong hand of Father's on my shoulder was one of
the greatest blessings of my life."

Willem's interest in spiritual matters was awakened very
early. On Sunday afternoons, he attended a young men's
club of the YMCA, where he soon had a leading part. When
he learned to play the organ, he became the organist for the
prison services on Sunday mornings.

During his college years, he became fascinated with the
Hebrew language. He managed to talk a Jewish boy into
giving him Hebrew lessons for ten cents for a whole afternoon. A love for the language of the Bible began to grow in
his heart. It would never leave him.

Wider Horizons

When Tante Jans started her Gospel work among soldiers, Willem became a great help to her. His horizons were
widened at a missionary conference, which he described in
a letter home.

I have discovered here that Barteljorisstraat 19 is not
the only place in the world where people really understand what counts. I am thrilled to see how the Holy
Spirit is at work in Indonesia. Isn't it beautiful to see
the same faith, which is so dear to us, being found a
few continents away?

The natural thing for Willem would have been to continue
in his father's footsteps and become a watchmaker. When
the time came, it was decided that he would give it a try, but

Here is a ten Boom family gathering. Each member had a special talent to contribute to the work of God which was done in the Beje.

after one week in the watch shop, Willem's decision was made. He told Father that he was not cut out for the watchmaker's trade, and he was going to be a minister.

Father said, "I told my dad the same thing, but he decided I was going to be a watchmaker, and that was that. I don't want to do the same thing to you. If you believe that God is calling you to be a minister, then you will study theology."

Mother wrote about Willem's decision in her diary:

October, 1901

The Lord has kept the children, and they are all prospering. Betsie is a great help in the shop. She is going to take a bookkeeping examination, and is helping her father with the books and other writing. She is taller than I am now, and we are all very happy with her.

Our Willem is also growing up fast. His life has taken quite a different course than we thought at first. We wanted to let him learn watchmaking, but soon saw that he was not happy with it. It was a difficult matter. After much prayer and serious consideration, we decided that he should go to high school instead of secondary school, and he is now in the second class. He is learning well, and so far he is glad this happened.

So Willem went to the University of Leiden. His studies added a new dimension of life to the Beje. Coming home on weekends, he would enthusiastically share his experiences in the family circle. Father used the opportunity to study several subjects with Willem, which provided them with many topics for discussion and deepened their already intimate relationship.

Silver Wedding

Mother and Father celebrated their silver wedding anniversary in 1909, while Willem was continuing his studies. Her diary entry for this time tells of her thankfulness for God's blessings in her life.

September 24, 1909

Tomorrow we begin our anniversary celebrations. I want to begin this entry with my husband, and tell him that he has been the best and only one for me. He has been so faithful, looked after me so patiently, and led me, and I have no words to describe it. Oh, I wish I had the gift to say it, and to say it well. May the Lord bless him for all his love and grant that we may stay together for many years to come.

How blessed we are in our children, because they love and trust us so much. How we have prayed for them from the very beginning, not only from their birth, but long before that time.

How lovely Betsie looked, with her pure face and fair curls. She has been a dear eldest daughter to us. May the Lord bless and keep her and make her very happy in her future life.

Then comes our son. He was greatly blessed during this past year. The Lord kept him through many dangers of soul and body. May God cause him to become a faithful servant of His. He has been a good son to us and good brother to the girls. When I look at other young people these days, I would not have him any different.

Nollie passed her examinations with good marks. She did not want to become a teacher, and is often rebellious, but she admits that the Lord is busy with her, and she is learning to follow.

Corrie is now at the Domestic Science school, and is having many experiences which are absolutely strange to her, especially with worldly matters and non-Christians. We are very much at peace about her, because we know she is in the Lord's hands and is in the world, but not of the world.

That Old Testament Feeling

When Willem completed his studies, the time came for him to enter the active ministry. I knew the ties of affection between him and the happy home could not remain as close as they had been. I wrote about it to a friend.

It seems so strange to us that Willem is going to leave home for his first position as an assistant pastor. After I had helped him pack his suitcases, we sat down at the dinner table, all looking a little depressed.

Father said, "Nobody needs to be sad about Willem's leaving. We know that he is going out into God's work. He has the full blessing of his father and mother."

Father's words gave me such an Old Testament feeling as I recalled how, in old times, the patriarchs blessed their children. What great value the paternal blessing had in those days. The father truly represented God in his family. Willem experienced this in a very real way.

Home in Made

Soon afterwards, Willem found a precious pearl. Tine van Veen, the young sister of Doctor van Veen, our family doctor, accepted Willem's proposal to become his life partner. Willem was minister in the small village of Made from

lem to the Barteljorisstraat during those days. There, in the living room behind the watch shop, they were brought daily before the throne of God.

Father was particularly affected by Willem's problems. He usually left the job of letter writing to the women of the family, but in such a time of crisis he wrote a warmhearted, personal letter to Willem and his wife.

June 24, 1919

My dear children,

We bring your needs daily before the throne, and we know that He who has all power will answer and reveal His glory, even using these difficulties.

As for you, I believe what is happening to you can be compared to an oak tree which is being violently shaken by a storm, but which therefore reaches down its roots even more firmly into the ground.

You have chosen to follow the Lord. He has given you grace so that your trumpet may not give an uncertain sound, with the result that you are now experiencing persecution and hatred. Satan is rearing his head and will certainly try you often.

God is holding your hand, so do not be anxious. A first battle like this is a big thing for a young recruit. However, this is a real school, and God is teaching you precious lessons. And it will not stay dark and difficult forever. Who knows how soon the Lord will give light and joy in your church?

Letter to a Doubting Theologian

Willem's letters to the Beje became more and more depressed. Both he and Tine felt isolated and lonely in Made, surrounded as they were by stony-hearted farmers. There

were many problems. But worse than that, Bible criticism
and doubt had slowly begun to eat away at Willem's faith.
There is a tone of unusual firmness in the letter which Willem received from Father during this time.

Dear Son,

Before I leave on a journey, I want to write to you
about a few things, and, at the same time, I want to do
whatever I can to express my love for you and your
family.

You know very well how we are all taking part in the
difficulties you are experiencing in Made. The main
thing I can do is to pray, and we are all doing that.

Now, Willem, you are my son, and you resemble me
in more ways than one. You may be sure that Satan
knows your weak points and will touch your Achilles'
heel in times of turmoil and despair. I also know how
hard it is when somebody tells you your faults, even if
it is your own father. When I write you the following, it
is because I love you and because I know you and
myself a little bit.

In your letters, I sense an undertone of doubt as to
whether the Bible is really and truly God's Word. Now
you can be sure, Willem, that Bible criticism will bring
death wherever it goes. Man's reasoning and the authority of the Bible seem to be irreconcilably opposed.

But is this not also the case with predestination and
man's responsibility? Is there only one truth in these
matters? Yes, I am sure there is! But here in this
earthly life, apparent contradictions will remain.

The ground on which we build our hope does not lie
in man's knowledge, but in God's faithfulness. Science, be it theology, philosophy, or history, undoubt-

edly has its value, but the words ". . . for we know in part . . ." apply, especially in this realm.

One day, in heaven, we will have complete insight and knowledge, but here below we have to grasp many things without fully understanding them. We have to make a clear choice between man's scientific criticism and the declaration, "It is written."

9

The Extended Vision

The four years that Willem and his family spent in Made were ones of fiery trial, but the hour of deliverance came. A call came from Zuylen, a picturesque little place only a few miles from the large city of Utrecht. Here, with a university a short distance away, Willem had opportunities for further study, for which the church allowed him one day a week.

Willem's vision began to extend far beyond the limits of the quiet, distinguished village of Zuylen. "We will not stay here too long," he said to Tine at their inauguration. "The missionary bug has bitten me!" The seeds planted in his heart during the missionary conferences he attended during his teenage years, and during the visits of the many missionaries who came to the ten Boom home, began to bear fruit. And one subject began to fascinate him in particular—Israel.

The Turning Point

"Tine, listen to this!"

Looking up from her cooking, Tine noticed the excitement in Willem's eyes as he came into the kitchen, waving a magazine.

"This is very interesting," he continued. "The Society for the Defense of the Christian Religion has announced a competition calling for a written study on the subject of anti-Semitism in Europe. Look, Tine, this is something that interests me. It may mean very little for my pastoral work, and it will not bring in any money, but the subject fascinates me. I would like to give all my spare time to such a study.''

Tine needed no further persuasion. She encouraged him at once. From then on, Willem's visits to the university became more and more frequent. As his study progressed, he said to Tine, "I was captivated by the subject of anti-Semitism from the start, but now that I am really getting into it, it is taking possession of me. I can no longer get away from it. The Jewish question is haunting me. It is so dangerous. Anti-Semitism has repercussions which will affect the whole world.''

As he plunged into a study of the European literature of the nineteenth and twentieth centuries, Willem discovered a dark, creeping power working underground in the European mind. It was a new form of anti-Semitism, which did not treat Judaism as a religion, but sought to condemn it on the principle of racism.

"The Jews are an inferior race," proclaimed French and German historians, philosophers, and scientists. The stage was being set for the most massive assault on the Jewish people in the history of the world.

These discoveries began to deeply affect Willem's inner life. He soon became known for his sermons about the Christian's responsibility toward the Jews and the organic unity of the Old and New Testaments. His prophetic messages usually went over the heads of the average churchgoers, whose scope of vision did not reach far beyond the towers of Utrecht, which they could see from their village.

When Willem's writings on the subject were published, they immediately drew the attention of the Dutch Society for Israel, founded in 1861 in Amsterdam. They rec-

Love for the Jewish people was handed down from generation to generation in the ten Boom family. During the Second World War, they showed this love through action. Here is Casper with some of those Jews.

ognized Willem's deep concern for Israel's plight. Willem received an urgent call: Would he consider entering into special service as a missionary to the Jewish people in Amsterdam?

A new subject for prayer was dispatched to the Barteljorisstraat in Haarlem. The whole family realized that this would be a great turning point in Willem's life. It would mean giving up the relatively stable financial security of a parsonage for what Tine called the shaky instability of a little-known society; exchanging the official position of a pastor for a difficult-to-define job as a missionary.

Willem was already too far involved to run away from his true calling. At this time, a letter from his father helped to tip the balance.

September 14, 1925

My dear children,

We want to let you know that we are sharing in your experience with all our hearts, and our prayers are continually mounting to God's throne for His guidance and blessing for you. If this is God's way, there are several noteworthy facts.

My father, who was a great admirer of Da Costa, was a life-long member of the Dutch Society for Israel. A portrait of Da Costa hung in our living room for as long as I can remember. A large number of workers for the cause of Israel have visited our home. When I lived on the Rapenburg in Amsterdam, I often used to speak to the Jews about the Messiah.

But all this is not the main thing. The most important matter is that for many years you have had a great love for the Hebrew language and now, through your response to the present wave of anti-Semitism, you have discovered in yourself a special love for God's own people.

So I do hope that it will come about, and that you will not only be blessed in this work and be a blessing, but that you will also find fulfillment and satisfaction in it.

A new period began in Willem's life. The Society for Israel insisted that he be well prepared for his work, and it was decided that he would take off one year for further study at the Institutum Judaicum in Leipzig, Germany. He had to leave his beloved Tine and four small children to become a student again.

The city of Leipzig must have had a special fascination for Willem, with his love for Bach's music. Besides, he was now at the hub of Germany's cultural life, an excellent place for him to study the subject that had already captivated him. His friends urged him to work it into a doctoral thesis.

Tine wrote in her diary, "My husband, who had no ambition about a doctorate, allowed the Holy Spirit to lead him to venture out into preparing a thesis."

It was a difficult undertaking. Between times of study, he had to give himself to his work and his family. But God blessed, and in 1928, Willem received his degree as doctor of philosophy. Vast opportunities now lay before him.

Identifying the Monster

I am holding in my hand a little black book from the old chest. Its cover is warped, and the binding cracks as I open the yellowed pages. The lengthy title is, *Entstehung des Modernen Rassenantisemitismus in Frankreich und Deutschland* (The birth of modern racial anti-Semitism in

France and Germany). It is Willem's doctoral thesis.

Willem began his studies on the subject in 1925. Germany was in deep turmoil. The First World War had left the country impoverished, confused, and split by inner factions. Marxism had failed to fulfill the expectations of the working class—the world revolution it had promised had not taken place. Instead, there was anarchy, weakness, and vacillation in the government. The country was sinking into moral decay.

At the same time, in the basement of the disillusioned German nation, the elements were being prepared which would lead to one of the starkest paradoxes of history. An Austrian painter would, some eight years later, take the reins of this sophisticated nation, and within a dozen more years, he would lead it to utter ruin, causing the deaths of untold millions, among them, six million Jews.

While Willem was writing his book in Leipzig, Adolf Hitler was in prison, dictating *Mein Kampf,* the book that contained the basis of his National Socialist revolution.

Willem wrote to Tine:

> I expect that in a few years' time, there will be worse pogroms than ever before. Countless Jews from the east will come across the border to seek refuge in our country. We must prepare for that situation.

This vision was going to pursue him for the rest of his life and propel him into preparing Holland's Christians for the coming events. From the pulpit and with his pen, Willem was going to warn the Dutch. Large-scale operations for rescuing Jews had to be organized. His own home had to be prepared for receiving the refugees. The events of the following years only proved how correct he had been in this vision.

Between Pastor's Study and Marketplace

Willem became a prolific writer. He was not an outstanding speaker, but through his books, he found an outlet for the message that burned in his heart. All his books, now no longer available, were related to the subject of Israel, and they contributed much to a better understanding of the Old Testament and God's plan for His people.

However, Willem was well aware of the danger of becoming a bookworm, a theoretician fleeing from life's reality into the remoteness of quiet study. He needed contact with people. His work with the Society for Israel called for his spending a few days every week in the marketplace of Amsterdam's Jewish quarter. He had lively discussions there with Jews from all walks of life, distributed Bibles and literature, and witnessed to everyone who would listen to what he told about the Messiah.

Following the old ten Boom tradition, Willem's house was open to everybody in need. The name of his house was *Theodotion,* which means "gift of God." It was surrounded by a large property, which allowed plenty of possibilities for expansion. Willem had a vision of a spacious center, where hospitality to the needy would be part of his ministry.

Tine often suppressed a sigh when more and more plates were added to the long table in the dining room, while household finances were constantly low. But Willem's optimistic faith in God's provision helped to turn the tide. He would answer Tine's worried comments by saying, "Enough for today, promises for tomorrow. What more do we need?"

Years later, my nephew Peter was visiting a synagogue in a suburb of Tel Aviv with a friend. At the end of the service, his friend introduced Peter to a Dutch Jew who had also attended.

"Do you happen to know the name ten Boom?" the Jew asked. He told that he had hidden in Willem's house during the Nazi occupation. "When the Gestapo came," he added, "I hid under the floor of Dr. ten Boom's study. When the soldiers came in, he started to scold them for disturbing his sermon preparation. The soldiers were intimidated by his self-confident manner and left him alone. Your uncle saved my life."

God's Orchestra

Willem's hope and expectation, and his view on Israel's calling, were clearly expressed in the following article that he wrote.

Years ago, while studying in Leipzig, I had the opportunity to attend a very special concert. Two hundred brass orchestras, from every part of the country, had come together. The director had the enormous task of uniting this huge group into one orchestra. It was no wonder that at the first rehearsal he laid down his baton with a gesture of despair after only a few bars.

However, he had anticipated this difficulty and was prepared for it. Behind him, on the platform, sat five of his own children. He had trained them thoroughly and practiced the program with them. Now he had them play. First they demonstrated how *not* to play the piece—the result was discord. Then they showed how it *should* be played. In no time, the other orchestras took over and order was brought out of chaos.

You understand the illustration. Israel received the

lessons firsthand and is then called upon to give a demonstration to the nations of the world. All through its history, God prepared Israel to show the world how a people should walk with God.

One day Israel will be the instrument to teach the whole world to worship and praise the Creator. This vision was clearly in the mind of the psalmist. "O Praise the Lord, all ye nations! praise Him, all ye people" (*see* Psalm 117:1).

Israel received the teaching according to the Torah, firsthand, but it is intended for the whole world, and if Israel neglects its vocation among the nations, it also receives the curse firsthand.

There is yet another aspect to Israel's calling. It bears in itself a reflection of the condition of the whole world. Israel's existence is directly related to the unity of the world's nations. Therefore it is the international people *par excellence.*

When the peoples of the world get together and unite, Jerusalem flourishes. It is the city which is patterned after world peace. On the other hand, if Israel is on the decline, the whole organism of humanity is in upheaval, and world peace languishes.

We see the world becoming more and more chaotic, but when other nations have ruined themselves by their deification of power and violence, the great inner change will begin with the Jews. Israel will then behold its Messiah, and a spirit of repentance will come upon them. Up to the present time, it has shown them how they should not behave. The result has been centuries of suffering and dispersion. This will usher in the great springtime for the world. The days of refreshment (see

Acts 3) will start, when Israel rediscovers its great missionary calling and its own ministry to the world. As a result, a great power toward worldwide renewal will flow forth from Israel in all directions. God's people will have found the fountain where sins are washed away—it will share its joy with the whole world and lead it in a symphony of praise to the Creator, the God of Israel.

In later years, Willem became more and more conscious of the fact that the witness to the Jews had to have a completely different character from the proclamation of the Gospel to the Gentiles. Was not Israel God's first love? And God's gifts and His call are irrevocable! Willem understood that God's plan for the Jew is not to abandon his Jewishness. Through a personal knowledge of Jesus as his Messiah, the Jew becomes a true son of Israel and already experiences the fulfillment of the divine promises. He becomes a "sample" of what one day will be Israel's collective, national experience.

This had always been Father's vision—Willem inherited it and worked it out theologically. In the course of time, he asked his society to take off the label *missionary*. He realized that Christians must approach Israel in an attitude of deep humility, listen to Israel, and learn from God's dealings with His people. Also, he became convinced that the witness to Israel was the task of the whole Church and should not be confined to a special society. The occupation of Holland was to bring this about. The Nazis immediately liquidated every organization working for and amongst Jews. Willem became pastor "on special service" and, as such, could continue his work in the service of the Dutch Reformed Church.

Besides, he never saw his activity as being limited to Jews only.

O let the nations be glad and sing for joy . . . . Let the people praise thee, O God; let all the people praise thee.

Psalm 67:4, 5

10
Father and I

"Comfort ye, comfort ye my people, saith your God. Speak ye comfortably to Jerusalem, and cry unto her, that her warfare is accomplished, that her iniquity is pardoned . . ."

Father was reading Isaiah 40. It was Sunday afternoon. He always read the Bible with us after every meal, but on Sundays he would work progressively through Isaiah 40–66.

Chapter 40:12: "Who hath measured the waters in the hollow of his hand and meted out heaven with a span . . . ?"

I knew it by heart. We heard it three times a year. The cadence of Isaiah belonged to the Sunday noon. Father's voice read it in a way which made it sound like that which it really was—a poem.

Through all the years that we lived together, Father shared my walk with the Lord. I feel so privileged when I look back on the time spent in the Beje. Our family was an advance troop in Jesus' army. Jesus was King of kings. Father was one of His captains.

When I think back to the time I was a toddler, I sometimes hear Father say, "Be a big girl. Don't cry!" Then he would take me in his arms, and I would feel his beard tickling my cheek. Walking over to the pictures on the wall as he held me, he would tell me interesting stories to distract my thoughts from my bumped head or skinned knee.

Every night before I went to sleep, Father would tuck me in. It was always a private moment for the two of us. I would talk over the events of the day, and I knew that the moment would soon come when he would say, *"Welterusten,* Correman. Sleep well. God loves you."

Then I would feel his big hand on my face. I wanted to preserve that happy feeling, so I did not move. I did not want to lose that comforting touch of Father's big hand.

Fifty years later, I lived in a part of the world where waking up and going to sleep were full of danger. I was in the prison of a cruel enemy, and nobody knew what the guards would do to us during the day or night.

I would close my eyes at night and say, "Heavenly Father, lay Your big hand on my little face for a moment." He did, and I would not want to move and lose that comforting touch of my heavenly Father's hand.

Because Father showed his love to me, he trained me to understand something of our heavenly Father's love. That was preparation for living. If you are the parent of a little child, please, show him your earthly love. You will help him to understand our heavenly Father's love when he needs it.

Are Your Children Saved?

An evangelist was a guest in our home once, and I heard him asking Father, "Mr. ten Boom, are all your children saved?"

"Praise the Lord, yes—all four of them. I can say that by the grace of God."

That evening, when I was alone with Father, I said, "Papa, you said that all four of us were saved. What did you mean by that?"

He answered with a question. "Correman, do you believe that Jesus died on the cross for your sins?"

"Yes, Papa. He died for the sins of the whole world, even mine."

"Do you love the Lord Jesus?"

"I do, Father. You know that."

"Do you believe that Jesus is in your heart?"

"I know He is."

"You see, my little girl, that is how I know that you are saved."

The Dream

I was well aware of my Christian heritage, and once had an interesting dream, which I found recorded in a letter to some of my friends.

Dear Girls,

Last night I had an interesting dream. The funny thing was, all during my dream, I was conscious that these things were happening many, many years before I was born. It was the time when my great-grandfather Gerrit was a gardener at the Bronstede estate. Father has often told me about this man's faith, courage, and patriotism.

I dreamed I was walking over a street rough with cobblestones. I had never had such an interesting adventure. The people I saw wore clothing different from what I had on. Old-fashioned carriages passed me. I realized that I was walking in the time when the princes of Orange still reigned in our country.

I saw an old inn at the side of the road and went in. Men were sitting there with broadbrimmed hats, smoking long pipes, and sitting on rough chairs beside windows with small windowpanes.

I did not say anything, but the people seemed to

know who I was, and the innkeeper said, "That man over there is Master ten Boom. I am sure you are interested in meeting him."

My forefather greeted me kindly, but did not seem amazed to see someone who would live a hundred years later. "Come with me," he said. "My wife will be glad to meet you."

Very quickly we were in his kitchen, where Great-grandmother was cooking a meal. They sat down at the table to eat, and I sat next to the window. A boy of about ten took off his cap, and they all prayed silently.

"Is that boy my grandfather?" I thought to myself.

After the meal, Great-grandfather took his Bible and read a portion. "Child," he said, "when your time to live comes, much will be different from what you see here around you. But this Book will be the same. If anyone undertakes to change it, then know that is wrong. The Word of God is the same for ever and ever."

He took my hand and led me to the garden. I saw how he put some seed into the earth. "This seed will give flowers. Before they die, they will give seed. It will go the same with the ten Booms. You will exist for many years after I have died. The seed of the Gospel message of the Bible brings forth fruit on and on. It will last."

This was the end of my dream, but I was strangely moved. I like what I dreamed about the Bible. "Heaven and earth will pass away, but God's Word will never pass away."

I was reading the Psalms for the first time.
"Father, have you the same Bible as I?"

"Yes, girl, all the Bibles are the same."

"But you have read the Psalms so often for us and now I read things I have never heard before. Listen, Daddy, Psalm 37:38: "But the transgressors shall be destroyed together: the end of the wicked shall be cut off."

Father smiled. I remember his answer.

"There are many things in the Bible that children cannot yet understand. That is why I did not read them."

Father's Bible reading was not just a habit. How he used it to teach us!

Where Do I Belong?

As a teenager, I took over many of the household duties, while Betsie worked with Father in the shop. My talents in housekeeping are described in a letter I wrote to Betsie and Nollie.

First of all, I want to tell you that we are all fine, except for Tante Anna, who has a toothache, and Tante Bet, who is feeling tired, and Father, who is still not very healthy, and Tante Jans, who did not sleep well, and Mother, who longs terribly for her little daughters, and the cat, who just attacked the dog of Mr. Loran.

I started to toast some bread, and sat down beside it in order not to forget it. Then I fell asleep. I don't know how long I slept, but when I awakened, there was a terrible stench in the room. There was nothing left of the piece of bread but a pitch-black thing. I left it in its place for a moment, and then I quietly hid it among the old crusts, for I was deeply ashamed.

Sunday morning in the ten Boom household meant church, and church often meant freezing for body and soul. In the cold cathedral, the only heat came from foot warmers containing burning coals. But for the faithful, missing the spiritual warmth of the long sermons was worse than shivering in their heavy winter overcoats.

In the theological world of Holland, there were many different currents of liberalism. Often there were quarrels over doctrine, which left the heads hot and the hearts cold. This situation often made it difficult for us children to know what to believe. Father's faith was the solid rock to which we clung.

In 1910 I wrote to my brother, Willem, "There are so many problems assailing me at this time that I cannot handle them. The interpretation of the liberal pastors sometimes gets me very confused. If I did not have Father, I would never manage."

Some years later, I sent another letter to Willem.

I feel there are plenty of dangers around us. They cause us to look for reality, for a living faith, some solid point in this ocean of influences. All the time we hear about Christian moral consciousness, denial of man's corrupt nature, and glorifying of man's intellect. In this atmosphere, many ministers are losing ground.

Maybe I am exaggerating a little but I feel a little out of balance, myself. I do not belong in our Reformed Church, nor in the Christian Reformed Church, and not at all with the Darbists. Also, the other smaller fundamentalist circles do not satisfy me. I have studied too much church history for that. But then, where do I belong?

Since the official church did not provide the fellowship that our family needed, home prayer meetings became the means of strengthening our ties with fellow Christians and finding spiritual nourishment. The newer fundamentalist churches did not enjoy a good reputation in the circles in which our family moved, since they were generally considered shortcuts toward a revival which should take place inside the state church itself.

Singing for the Lord

However, I was discovering that the one way to avoid confusion is to become active in serving the Lord. Tante Jans had set us an example with her evangelistic meetings for soldiers. Since both Nollie and I had quite good singing voices, we were soon engaged in this Gospel work, and sang duets in the meetings. My feelings about my life at that time are reflected in another letter to my friends.

Dear Girls,

When I think about my life, it does not seem very important on the outside. I make the breakfast, wash the dishes, cook, sew, and in spare moments, I study a little Latin grammar as I watch the spluttering meat pan. This is my life at the moment, and I am happy in it. The only thing that casts a shadow is the misery in the world around us.

Every week, on Tuesday nights, I have a small part in the glorious work of bringing the Gospel to several hundred people. I sing at a Gospel meeting. Sometimes I stand there with my heart beating wildly and my voice trembling, and look only at the book. At those moments, it is such a comfort to me that God's strength is made perfect in weakness.

At other times, especially when Nollie and I sing together, my heart beats quite normally, and I enjoy singing. When the song has ended, and not until then, I look at the people. Then it does not matter if I grow nervous. I read lovely things in their eyes!

Willem felt very responsible for his sisters in this unusual work. I found a letter that I had written to him.

Dear Willem,

On Monday of last week, we sang in the military barracks. In order to oppose our efforts, they had not said that an army chaplain was going to speak, but had told the men that a singing comedian would perform. There were about four hundred soldiers present when we arrived, and they were not the type that would like a Gospel program.

When the pastor announced a hymn and distributed songbooks, the soldiers began to howl like wild animals. The pastor prayed, but hardly anyone could hear him, although he had a good, clear voice.

He then asked us to sing, and when we began, it became dead quiet. We sang the whole song, and they really listened. It was so strange and so wonderful, seeing a group of half devils come under the power of two weak girls.

Willem, as this was going on, we remembered that you did not agree with our doing this, and I can understand why you do not like the idea of us on a platform in the middle of such a place, but I am glad we did it.

We must not hide our light under a bushel. Although I am not looking for trouble. I shall do all I can when I am called by the Lord.

Although I very much enjoyed singing for the Gospel meetings, I was not yet convinced that it was proper for a woman to preach. This was an important issue in the church at the time, and I wrote Willem about my feelings on the matter.

> Pastor B. sent me a request to preach on December 12. I discussed it with Father and, following his advice, I declined the invitation.
>
> In the course for evangelists, we did not agree on the question whether the woman of our present day may preach or not. Father says that it will cause me to lose my femininity; I am seventy-five percent in agreement with him, but would like to have your opinion on this.
>
> This urge to evangelize—to tell people the glorious message of the Gospel—gives me a deep longing to speak out aloud, in the same way that it is so thrilling to sing out the message in the Grote Kerk as loudly as I can. But regarding this last matter, I am afraid there is some vanity connected with it.

Obviously, I eventually changed my mind about the propriety of a woman teaching the Gospel! For the time being, I settled for singing and teaching my sister Betsie's Sunday-school class when she was out of town. Here is my report to her after my first Sunday-school lesson:

> Oh, Betsie, how I miss you, especially at the Sunday school. The story did not go well, It is high time I started some teacher training. I wanted to explain to the children the meaning of "Feed my lambs," and asked them if they had ever seen a flock of sheep.
>
> "Yes, I have," said one. "My father is a lamb butcher."

I began to think of all the skinned sheep the boy's father worked with, and my inspiration vanished!

Another boy started to wave his arms enthusiastically every time I used the word fishing, so I had to give him the opportunity to tell what was on his heart. He explained that his father was a fisherman and caught huge fish, indicating with his arms how big the fish were. This was a signal for all the others to stretch out their arms and tell about the large fish that their fathers, brothers, or uncles had caught!

A New Career

The time came when Betsie and I switched roles. She had always worked in the shop, while I helped with the housekeeping. Finally, I decided I would like to learn the art of watch repairing. Father and I talked about it. He was known as the best watchmaker in Holland, and had written a booklet about the regulation of precision watches.

His father had taught him all he could, but Grandfather was more practiced in the art of clock repair than watch repair. Therefore he sent his son to Hoü, an internationally known watch repairer, to learn the trade. Father always talked with great respect about his teacher.

"Girl," he said, "I trust that you will become a more able watch repairer than your father."

We were standing in the living room as we had our talk, and Tante Anna overheard us as she came in with a basketful of clean laundry. "Casper," she said, "if Corrie becomes your helper, you will find that she never does one thing at a time. She will be your business associate, plus this, that, and the other. She will always be interested in twenty things at once."

Father smiled. He had never been too successful with his apprentices. The boys were not always willing to learn, and Father did not know how to teach them the trade. He used them more as errand boys and general helpers.

Soon after that talk, I started working with Father. I had my own workbench in the shop, and Father and I became more of a team than ever.

Much conversation went on in the shop. Mr. West kept the books of our business in his spare time. He was a sergeant-major, and always came to the shop in uniform. One day, I heard him talking to Father.

"Yes, but, Mr. ten Boom . . . ."

"Tell me, what is your *yes, but* this time?"

"I do not feel that I am saved."

"Does the Bible tell us that we are saved by feelings?"

"No sir, by faith."

"Have you received Jesus as your Saviour?"

"Yes, I have."

"And what happened then? The Bible says that whoever believes in the Son has everlasting life. Believe in the Lord Jesus Christ and you will be saved."

When Mr. West left, I said to Father, "Mr. West had exactly the same *yes, buts* as he had last week and two weeks ago. I think you have a lot of patience."

"Girl, doesn't the Lord have a lot of patience with me and with you?"

That evening, I had difficulty in repairing a very small watch. Just when it was almost ready, I broke a part. "Papa, please help me. I have broken the balance of the watch."

"You know there is nobody in the world I would rather help than my own daughter," was his kind answer.

Casper ten Boom saw the patience required in watchmaking as a part of his training by the Lord in the fruit of the Spirit. He felt privileged to have such a job.

I had to go back to him three times. "I am so sorry, Papa, but I have broken it again!"

"Give it to me. I will help you."

"Papa, where did you get your patience?"

"Girl, we have a privileged job. There is nothing like watch repairing for learning patience. And don't forget that patience is a fruit of the Spirit."

Father was an artist in his trade, but making money was not his strongest point. There were some ways in which I could give him advice. "Papa, why do you close the shop windows in the evenings? Far more people walk through the Barteljorisstraat at that time than during the day."

"I never thought of that. Go ahead. Whenever you see a way to improve the business, do it."

I saw that our stock of watches and clocks was insufficient and bought more than Father had ever purchased. Soon he left that side of the business in my hands. It went better than before, but what a lot of money problems we had to solve! Prayer with all the workers in the morning helped us to cast our burdens on the Lord, and during the day we often went to the living room and had a short extra prayer session with the rest of the family.

Shortly after I started to work in the shop, I realized that I needed extra training. "Papa, too often when a broken watch is brought in, I have to ask you or the watchmaker what the problem is. I would like to know more about the insides of a watch."

But in those days, the only place where watchmakers' schools existed was in Switzerland. How could Father ever afford to send me there?

A pocket watch which played ''Ranz des Vaches,'' a Swiss folk song. Casper's sale of this watch made it possible for Corrie to go to Switzerland to learn watchmaking.

11
Switzerland

dark. He was so enthusiastic that he brought in all his alarm clocks, watches, and even his guns to have illuminating marks put on them. A few days after Father wrote the article about ''Ranz des Vaches,'' this customer came into the shop.

''Mr. ten Boom, I would like to have a watch that nobody else has. Do you know if that is possible? I do not mind what the price is.''

''I know a watch that is unique,'' Father answered. ''It is the 'Ranz des Vaches.' '' He described the watch, and the man immediately took a large sum of money from his pocket. There were more bank notes on the showcase than I had ever before seen in our house.

"May I see the watch?" Father asked. He opened the watch, took his looking glass from his pocket, and adjusted something. "Your watch is very good. There was a little mistake, which I could easily put right. Will you please give me back the watch I just sold you? Young van Houten is a very good watchmaker. You can trust him."

The gentleman looked amazed, but he returned the watch he had just bought, and Father gave him back his money.

How could Father do that? Why? Had he forgotten the bill that was going to arrive? Father opened the door for the man and bowed in his courteous way.

"Papa, why did you do that?" I asked impatiently.

"Listen, girl, you know I brought the Gospel at Houten's funeral. What if that young man should hear one of his best customers went to ten Boom? Do you think the name of the Lord would be glorified? Corrie, there is blessed and unblessed money. I know you are thinking of the bill that has to be paid, but trust the Lord."

That evening I corrected Father's copy for his watchmakers' magazine. Betsie and I always did that, and it taught me a lot. In his article, Father described an unusual project which Betsie and I enjoyed reading. The emperor of Austria had ordered a special watch made for him. However, he had since abdicated, and could not afford the high price of the watch. It was of heavy gold, and was the first pocket watch ever made that played a tune. The tune was "Ranz des Vaches," a folk song. At the end of the article, Father wrote, "I congratulate the watchmaker who will sell this watch, most expensive in the world."

One of the customers who always went to Father's workbench was an officer who was very interested in the new discovery whereby watches could be...

Broke? No!

That was my first thought as I jumped out of bed. What a nightmare! The whole night, I had seen the bill that was due the next day. The bank manager had said he could wait only one more week, but the money was not there—neither in cash nor in the bank.

"Lord, please send many people to buy watches!"

That day, Father opened the door for a man whom I had never seen before. Sitting behind my workbench, I could hear part of their conversation.

"I need a good watch," the gentleman said.

Father had a persuasive way of describing a good watch. "This is a watch from one of the best factories, The steel is of the finest quality. You can trust it to give you the correct time, and you will have a watch you will enjoy for many years."

I saw the man take money from his wallet. Cash! What a joy. I was sure it would be enough to pay the bill. The man lingered for a moment before leaving the shop. What was he saying to Father? I leaned forward to hear.

"I had a good watchmaker, van Houten. He died some weeks ago, and his son now has the business. That young man is not a good watchmaker. I bought a watch from him, but it does not work properly. I took it back to him three times."

"I am going to Switzerland this week, and I will fetch the watch from the factory myself," the man said.

In Switzerland, the happy manufacturer showed our customer some other unusual watches, which he also bought. All the discount was sent to Father.

"Father, how wonderfully the Lord has helped us. I feel so ashamed that I was so scared."

The sale of the most expensive watch in the world brought in so much money that Father was able to send me to Switzerland as an apprentice in two factories. I would learn how to make the most important parts of watches. "When you can make something, you can repair it," Father said.

My Stay in Switzerland

I began the long journey to Switzerland. I reached Basel on the first day and had to wait there until the next day, when I could go on to Biel, my destination. I was so used to talking everything over at home that I almost told the hotel doorman where I was going when I went for a walk!

Business friends of Father's had found a room for me in a minister's home in Biel. Five boys, all students at the watchmakers' school, were also in the house. I started working in the watch factory.

What a contrast! I could picture Father behind his workbench in the corner of the small workshop. He and I would be busy for many hours each day, doing the meticulous work of repairing and cleaning watches. Although it was precision work, it did not always demand too much thought. Father and I both had Bibles in the drawers of our worktables, and he was always willing to talk over any problems which came into my busy brain.

There were happy interruptions, too. Betsie might come

into the shop, saying, "Father, Corrie, give your watches half an hour's rest. Mengelberg is playing a Bach cantata over the radio. Come into the living room, and in the meantime you will enjoy a cup of soup such as you have never tasted in your life." Father and I never refused. We enjoyed life.

Now I was sitting in a small factory, with Swiss people around me who had quite accepted the fact that they were cogs in a machine. They did the same little thing over and over again, hour in, hour out—sometimes all their lives. One of the workers had her seventieth birthday and received her pension. She went home, but after a week, she was back, begging to be allowed to go on with her work. She worked in the factory until she died. She had to put screws into holes all day long. The same-sized screw, the same-sized hole—thousands every day.

A Dutch Girl in a Swiss Factory

"Why? How could you? What is the meaning of this?" the director's voice demanded.

I stood in front of the factory owner and gasped for breath.

For about seven hours, I had done nothing but make curves in spiral watch springs—one after the other, again and again. Suddenly the door opened, and a big dog ran into the room. I jumped up and hugged the dog. We fell onto the floor together and a happy fight started between us. One moment he was underneath me, the next moment I was trying to stop his tugging and loosening all my hair over my laughing face. I don't know who enjoyed the fight more.

And then the director came in. I felt like a naughty schoolgirl as I stood in front of him. His face was one big question mark. "Why?"

"Because I am not part of an engine," I replied. "This is the fifteenth day I have been making curves in spiral springs for nine hours a day. Your dog was a most welcome guest, and perhaps he saved me from going crazy."

Did the director understand the Dutch girl standing in front of him, her hair all over her face, her dress very crumpled after a fight with his dog?

"I spent nine hours a day for *two years* of my life, making that curve," he replied.

"Which years of your life were they?"

"When I was sixteen and seventeen."

"Forgive me, sir, but you are Swiss. I am Dutch!"

Do Not Refuse the Cross

Even the beginning of the day in Switzerland was different from that in the Beje. Breakfast was dry bread and chocolate milk. What a combination! I felt hungry the whole morning.

Sometimes there was shopping to do, and I enjoyed serving the company by going to the shop and buying gasoline or whatever was needed. I always bought some good Swiss buns at the same time and returned through a back street, where I would eat them on the steps of a house. I would look around to be sure nobody from the factory was passing by to see the Dutch apprentice wasting her time.

Although I had passed my twentieth birthday, I often behaved like a teenager. The Haarlem mayor's daughter, Stanny, was at a school in Biel to learn French. I knew her from the shop, and on several evenings we went for walks outside Biel and had a good swim in the lake. After ten o'clock, the front door of the minister's home over the church was closed. One evening, Stanny and I forgot all about the time, enjoying the moonlight over the lake of Biel.

The front door was closed. I did not want to ring the bell,
for the minister would see that I had broken a rule of the
house. One window in the church was open, and I tried to
climb up to reach it. If I stood on Stanny's shoulders, I
could manage. It was almost a success. I reached the window, leaned over the edge—but not quite far enough—and
fell back, nearly into the arms of the minister, who was
coming around the corner. Stanny had disappeared.

At the breakfast table the next morning, the minister said,
"Although all of you work on watches, one of you could not
read the clock last night. I hope this will not happen again."

Contact with home kept me encouraged. Streams of letters came and went. I wrote that the French language was
causing me difficulties. The factory manager's little girl
often came into our workroom. She and I understood each
other, and I learned simple French from her. Father wrote:

> I am glad you have that little girl to practice your
> French with. Talk as much as you can with her. She
> will understand your broken French better than the
> grown-ups. You asked me in your letter why we always
> have so many sorrows and money problems. Here
> is a legend from my notebook.
>
> Two pilgrims were on their way to a city that they
> had to reach by nightfall. Each of them was carrying a
> cross that was so heavy they nearly fell under the
> weight of it.
>
> One of them took his cross and sawed half of it off.
> He comforted himself with the thought that it was still a
> cross. The other sawed through the beams lengthwise,
> so that they became half as thick. He thought, "It does
> not matter. The shape is the same."
>
> At last they reached their destination, but they could

not enter the city. A deep canal blocked the way. There was no bridge, no boat or ferry.

"Our crosses will help us out," they thought. "We will use them as a bridge."

So the first one laid his cross across the water, but it was too short. The other one's cross fitted exactly from one bank to the other, but when they tried to step on it, it began to crack. It was too thin to hold them. There they stood, regretting that they had made their crosses lighter.

We must be so careful that we do not refuse the cross that the Lord has given us to carry. Let us remember that our present sufferings serve to prepare us for entering into the Kingdom of the Lord Jesus Christ. Jesus said, "And whosoever doth not bear his cross, and come after me, cannot be my disciple" (Luke 14:27).

My French Teacher

The only language used in the minister's house and at the factory was French. How difficult it was for me to understand. I decided to take French lessons, and Miss Bonjour became my teacher. In her little house, I found the fellowship that kept homesickness at bay.

We read the Bible together, and every week she took me on a picnic. She always had the best Swiss cheese and chocolate in her knapsack. Mountains in Switzerland are difficult to climb, but old Berta Bonjour had Swiss legs, and although I was much younger, I had difficulty keeping up with her.

We stretched out in the grass of an alpen meadow, a field with flowers all around us. There was a tremendous view over the lower mountains to the Alps, with their eternal snow. Berta got out her little Bible and started to read about Jesus' coming again.

"But as to the times and the seasons, brethren, you have no need to have anything written to you. For you yourselves know well that the day of the Lord will come like a thief in the night" (*see* 1 Thessalonians 5:1, 2).

"I don't know much about the future," Berta said. "My minister speaks about it once a year. Do you know what the Bible tells about it?"

"Father taught much, Berta," I said. "And when he prays, he always ends the prayer with the same words: 'And, heavenly Father, let the day come soon when Jesus, Your beloved Son, comes on the clouds of heaven.' Even when I was a little girl, I knew that must be a great joy, because Father prays for it every day."

"I never thought about the joy," said Berta. "I am a little afraid of Jesus' coming."

"Do you go to church?"

"Yes."

"If you are trusting Jesus Christ, you have nothing to fear. Since Jesus finished all on the cross, the judgment day will not be terrible. If we believe in Jesus, we will be saved."

The more I got to know Berta, the more I enjoyed the talks I had with the old saint. She loved the Lord. She had been governess of the children of the Earl von Moltke in Germany, and now she lived on a very small income in her miniature Swiss chalet. I learned from her how poor people could be rich when they had the gift of sharing the little they have with others.

Factory Training

I slowly became used to life in a factory. Swiss people demand much of their workers. I had to keep a strenuous schedule, but I enjoyed the company of the people around me.

Later I understood that working in the factory was part of my training, and I remembered Father's legend. More than thirty years later, I was once again a factory worker, this time as a prisoner in the hands of Adolf Hitler.

Everybody was trained to make the lives of prisoners as difficult as possible. However, I learned to almost appreciate the work we had to do in that factory, making radio sets for German airplanes. As long as I was in the factory, my life was almost the normal life of a factory worker. What a good thing it was that when I was young, I had learned about factory life!

Back to the Beje

I returned to the Beje and the business, and there followed many fruitful years of work in the watch shop and outside. Father knew the art of living, and passed it on to us. He wrote this letter to me when I was out of town:

My dear child,

We had a beautiful Sunday today. It was a foretaste of heaven. A Sunday like this is a peaceful island amid the wild, unruly waves of the ocean. Tomorrow we set sail again from this quiet harbor. Then we will head into battle against the storm of cares.

Sometimes, during the night, I think about my problems and my lack of money, but then the light glows inside me. He who is holding the rudder will bring everything to a good end.

12

Father and His Grandchildren

Father loved children, and they loved him. His three daughters and one son had grown up and become more like teammates than people who needed his help, but there were other little ones—his grandchildren. He wrote about them in his notebook.

As to my children, I have the glad assurance that they belong to the Lord. It is my burning desire, more than I could ever express, that one day I will meet my grandchildren, whom I love so much, before the throne of God.

Mother's health deteriorated soon after my sister Nollie married. Mother had so enjoyed Willem and Tine's little ones. Her visits to their home were high points in her life.

Happily, Nollie did not move far away. Flip, her husband, became director of a school that Father helped start on the other side of Haarlem, and they lived near it with their six children.

Father was on the school board and worked closely with his son-in-law. The grandchildren were a source of joy to him, and he went to visit Nollie and her family every Sunday afternoon.

A year before we were arrested, Nollie was imprisoned because two Jews were found in her house. She was taken

Casper wrote to his wife, "I become more and more convinced that the Lord granted me an overwhelming privilege when He gave you to me."

to a prison in Amsterdam in a prison van, in which she had to stand in a small square compartment. It was pitch dark, but suddenly there was a beam of light, and she wrote the words, "Jesus is Victor" on the wall with a lead pencil she had hidden under her hair.

She was taken to a huge police station in Amsterdam, where they pushed her into a basement cell without any light. She started to sing, and when she heard a voice say, "However can you sing?" she realized she was not alone.

The other woman started to cry. Nollie said, "Don't lose courage. God is still on the throne. We are not alone."

Nollie was later released through the help of a German doctor. I seldom saw Father so happy as the moment he held her in his arms again.

Most of the people who were mentioned in these old letters are no longer alive, but I talked to Peter and Bob, two of Father's grandchildren, and they gladly shared their memories of him.

Gladly, Lord

One day, when Bob was a small boy, he accompanied his grandfather to a bus stop. As they waited for the bus to come, Bob said, "Grandpa, you are so old, and you may have to die one day. Do you really want to go to heaven?"

"Oh, my boy," was the reply, "I have such dear children, and such lovely grandchildren, and there are so many beautiful things to enjoy in this world, so I do not really want to go yet. But, Bob, if God should call me today and say, 'Casper, come!' I would answer, 'Gladly, Lord!' "

First the Help, Then the Talk

"How are your mathematics coming, Bob?" Father asked his grandson one day. "I pray for them every day."

Bob looked up into the gently smiling face and thought, "Does Grandpa take time to pray for my mathematics?"

Father was very good at encouraging his grandchildren, at stimulating positive things in other people. Once Bob came to the watch shop and showed Father a beautiful illustrated book that he had just bought at Mr. Vernhout's store.

Father admired it and asked, "How were you able to buy this nice book?"

"Oh," Bob said, "Mr. Vernhout told me I could pay off a little bit every month. I will have it paid for in six months."

At this, Father went to the money box in the workshop, took out the amount needed to pay for the book in full, and gave it to Bob. "Here," he said, "take this and run to the shop to pay for the book. Promise me one thing, however—that you will never again buy anything without paying for it straightaway. In that way, you will be kept from getting into debt." Bob appreciated the fact that Father gave him the money first and then gave the lecture.

Casper ten Boom with six of his grandchildren.

Poffertjes' Day

Poffertjes' Day took place once a year. This was a tradition Father started, and his grandchildren looked forward to the great occasion for weeks. When at last the big day arrived, they would all stand waiting in front of one of Haarlem's special poffertjes restaurants.

Finally, Father would appear, all smiles. He took the children inside, and the feast began. Poffertjes are little pancakes, served with butter and powdered sugar. What a treat it was for the grandchildren, and how Father enjoyed seeing them feast on this delicious dish. He was every inch a grandfather.

Father gave his grandchildren a feeling of security. There was something rocklike about him that made them feel safe. Peter remembers the hours he spent sitting on a little stool in the workshop, learning to type on the old office typewriter. He loved the atmosphere of the shop, imagining that hundreds of clocks hung on the walls around him. The sound of the ticking and chiming, and the sight of his grandfather bending over his workbench, are still very clear in his mind.

The grandchildren never saw Father angry. Peter once asked, "Does Grandpa ever get angry?"

"No," we said, "but he does get a little annoyed if the soup is served too hot to eat."

The Queen's Day

The highlight of life in Haarlem was the yearly celebration of the Queen's birthday. Everybody dressed up, and the children wore costumes. A platform, covered with beautiful carpets and flowers, would be erected on the Grote Markt, the large marketplace in the center of town.

The mayor, councillors, and leading townspeople would assemble on the platform, and everybody else gathered in the marketplace.

Often on such occasions, Father was the special guest of the mayor, and a place was reserved for him on the platform. On this particular Queen's Day, Father rode to the marketplace in an open horse-drawn carriage. Hundreds of schoolchildren lined the streets, singing, shouting, and waving their flags at the old man with the silk top hat.

Suddenly, a shrill, excited child's voice could be heard above the noise, "Grandfather, Grandfather!" The coachman was ordered to stop, and the whole procession came to a standstill.

Father had spotted his little grandson Peter, and he quickly motioned to the boy to climb up into the carriage. When they arrived at the marketplace, Father took Peter by the hand, stepped through the crowds to the platform, and up the steps on the beautiful carpet.

The little boy knew he would never have been allowed on that wonderful place by himself, but now he was firmly holding his grandfather's hand. The policemen in front stepped back respectfully for Haarlem's grand old man and his grandson.

Peter remembers this incident as an example of what God does for His children. Of ourselves, we have no right to a victorious, free life, or to eternal life in heaven's glory. Yet God stooped down to us in His Son Jesus Christ. He took us by the hand and became the way for us to reach a place we could never reach by ourselves.

Mr. Kan

Father's shop was halfway down the Barteljorisstraat, and a little further on, on the opposite side of the street, was another watch shop. It belonged to Mr. Kan, a Jew.

The grandchildren were fascinated by Mr. Kan's shop window. It was always full of bright, shiny watches. In between, there were advertisements announcing super-special bargains. A slogan was mounted above the shop: *Wat Kan kan kan Kan alleen,* which is a clever play on words in Dutch that means, "Only Kan can do what Kan can do." Mr. Kan sold many more watches than Father.

One day Peter accompanied Father on one of his walks through town. He loved doing this, because people would often stop to look back at the dignified old man, and Peter was very proud of his grandfather.

As they walked through the Barteljorisstraat, they passed Mr. Kan's watch store. Peter looked at Father and said, "Grandpa, Mr. Kan is your competitor, isn't he?"

Father stopped and thought for a moment. "No, my boy, Mr. Kan is not my competitor. He is my colleague. And do not forget, he belongs to God's chosen people."

Peter was too small to understand about the Jewish people, but he understood that the Jews must be very special people, because of what he heard from his grandfather so many times.

Your Feet on the Rock

Father had a personal concern for each one of his grandchildren, and he did his part in preparing them for life. He rarely preached to them—his life spoke much louder than his words. Only once does Peter remember Father dealing with him directly about the need for salvation.

Peter was seventeen, and his whole interest was focused on his musical career. He thought he had no time for the things of God. One requirement for obtaining his diploma as an organist was that he had to work in an organ factory for a few weeks.

Before he left, Father had a talk with Peter. "My boy," he said, "you are going to have a new experience. You will be working among many different kinds of people in the factory. You will be exposed to temptations there which you have not had before. I am very concerned about how you will be able to resist. Peter, you need to make sure that you have your feet on the rock, that you know Christ as your Saviour."

Peter was not too willing to listen to his grandfather, but Father's words stuck in his mind, and he was not able to forget the incident.

About a year later, in disobedience of Nazi orders, Peter played the "Wilhelmus," Holland's national anthem, in the church where he was organist. He was put in prison for doing this.

During that month behind bars, God spoke to Peter again and again through a little New Testament smuggled in to him by his mother. It was then that Peter opened his heart to the Lord Jesus and received Him as his personal Saviour. Father's prayers had a part in preparing Peter for this experience.

The Future Is Perfectly Clear

The last letter of Father's which we have in our possession was written to one of his grandchildren. It is dated December 23, 1943, and gives us a little glimpse of what went on in the Beje just two months before the Gestapo found out about the hiding place.

My greatly beloved grandson,

Although I am quite lazy when it comes to letter writing, I want to answer your letter. There is not much news here. The war continues to rage outside. From that side we are shaken and plagued by all kinds of sad and troubling rumors. On the other hand, here inside the house we rejoice in a great many glorious experiences. We are protected and blessed here by a most extraordinary providence.

Your aunts and I are enjoying good health, and we have enough to eat. Yes, when I think it all over, we are enjoying abundance. I have nothing to complain about. I am only sorry that I can do so little work on my watches. I am too weak to work much, and my hands are not always steady.

But after all, I have had my time in the shop, and the new life I am now living is also good.

I receive every day as an undeserved gift. I only hope that I will be able to enjoy seeing, with all my faculties, the deliverance of our people and our fatherland. At any rate, I have so much to be thankful for! I am enjoying God's favor, and the future is perfectly clear.

The School of Faith

At the time that Father wrote Bob this letter, Peter was in hiding a few streets away from the Barteljorisstraat. He had to stay inside during the day, because the German soldiers picked up all the young men and sent them to Germany to help in the arms industry.

The only time Peter dared to leave his hiding place was in the evening. By walking through a few narrow streets, he could reach the alley which led to the side door of the Beje.

On the evening of February 28, 1944, Peter took this back

route to the Beje, intending to enjoy the companionship of the house and practice his piano. At the side door of the watch shop, he rang the bell three times, so we would know it was somebody from the family. A man opened the door to an unusually darkened hallway.

"You had better go upstairs. There are visitors in the dining room," the man said.

Peter climbed the winding stairway and reached the large front room, where the piano was. Some men, who were unknown to him, were sitting around the fireplace. They looked at Peter and asked him to sit down with them for a moment.

"We are friends of your grandfather and aunts," they explained. "Some of our friends in the underground have been caught. We are making plans to get them out of prison, but we have no weapons. Do you know where to find some?"

Peter knew at once that something was wrong. No underground worker would talk like this to a complete stranger. "I'm sorry," he replied, "I know nothing about weapons. If you don't mind, I have to leave."

Peter found himself looking into the barrel of a pistol. He was in the hands of the Gestapo. The enemy had struck the hiding place—were the Jews safe?

Peter was taken to the police station with the rest of us. Lying among all the other prisoners, he could not help thinking, "Lord, where were Your angels?"

Yet, every time he looked at his grandfather, he saw only peace on the face of the old man. Father was pale and weak, and Peter knew he might never see him again, but he heard Father's strong voice reading Psalm 91, and he was comforted.

Thou shalt not be afraid for the terror by night; nor
for the arrow that flieth by day; Nor for the pestilence
that walketh in darkness; nor for the destruction that
wasteth at noonday. A thousand shall fall at thy side,
and ten thousand at thy right hand; but it shall not
come nigh thee. Only with thine eyes shalt thou behold
and see the reward of the wicked. Because thou hast
made the Lord, which is my refuge, even the most
High, thy habitation; There shall no evil befall thee,
neither shall any plague come nigh thy dwelling. For he
shall give his angels charge over thee, to keep thee in
all thy ways.

Psalm 91:5–11

Boom Is Dutch for *Tree*

Two months later, Peter, Nollie, and Willem were released from prison, and Peter learned that his grandfather
had passed from the prison hospital to the glories of heaven.

For weeks after, there was no news from Betsie and me.
As the days dragged by, it became clear to the family that
we would have a much more severe punishment than the
others.

Then, one morning, Nollie burst into Peter's room, with
tears streaming down her face. "Peter," she cried, "we
have just received news that both Corrie and Betsie have
been transported to a concentration camp in Germany.
Father died in prison, and now I am going to lose my two
sisters!"

Peter was speechless. What could he say to comfort his
mother? He knew how hard life would be for us in the
concentration camp. When Nollie left the room, he fell to
his knees. "Lord, give me a word from You. Show me Your
side of the situation."

He opened the Bible and read.

Blessed is the man that trusteth in the Lord, and whose hope the Lord is. For he shall be as a tree planted by the waters, and that spreadeth out her roots by the river, and shall not fear when heat cometh, but her leaf shall be green; and shall not be careful in the year of drought, neither shall cease from yielding fruit.

See Psalm 1:1–3

With the open Bible in his hand, Peter ran downstairs to share the Scripture with his mother. They both knew that God was working out His own perfect, loving plan for Betsie and me.

Over thirty years have passed since that day. Now, looking back, we can see so much more of God's wisdom and love in His dealings with our family.

A tree planted by the riverside does not just happen to be there. Someone planted and prepared its place and knew why the tree had to grow on that very spot. As I have recalled these incidents about Father, my heart has filled with gratitude. I saw the hand of the One who planted this family in Haarlem, who kept it through the years of drought and suffering, fed it with His Word, and caused it to bear fruit. And perhaps it is not without significance that Boom is Dutch for *tree*.

Yad Va Shem

Yad Va Shem, Jerusalem—a place of sad memories. On the floor of the building are big, flat stones, with the names of concentration camps upon them. Ashes from bodies found in each camp are buried under each stone—a dark picture of one of the darkest events of this age.

There is an avenue of trees outside the building, called The Avenue of the Righteous. At the base of every tree is the name of the person who planted it—non-Jews who, at great risk, helped save Jewish lives during the war.

In 1968, I was invited to plant a tree on that boulevard. There is a flame burning day and night in the building. It says, "Do not forget." I turned a handle, and the flame burned brighter.

A man sang a litany in memory of Father, Betsie, Willem, and Kik, the four people in my family who died as a result of their work in saving Jews. I looked around me. Many Jewish children were standing on the balcony, and official state representatives stood next to me. Was there ever such sadness as on the faces in Yad Va Shem?

My thoughts turned away from the people who had been killed, to the ones who had been saved because God used my family, friends, and me. I heard my Father's voice say, "If I die in prison, it will be an honor to have given my life for God's ancient people."

Sad joy entered my heart. I prayed, "Dear Lord, by Your Holy Spirit, show me things from Your point of view." Was it possible to feel joy, to praise the Lord, at such a sad moment? Was I the only one here who could praise the Lord?

I saw, high up in the building, openings on four sides of the walls. Suddenly, hundreds of birds flew inside the hall. They sang, they chirped, they praised the Lord in their own way. I felt one with them.

"Father, Betsie, Willem, Kik—you gave your lives for God's chosen people," I whispered.

That day at Yad Va Shem I gave a talk about my father. I spoke of what he had meant to me, to all of his family, and even to strangers who saw God's love mirrored in the most difficult of circumstances. Here is part of my talk:

> Some time ago, I had an accident in the street of my hometown, Haarlem. A policeman helped me into a car and asked me my name.
>
> "Corrie ten Boom," I answered.
>
> "Are you one of those ten Booms whom we had to arrest twenty-two years ago?"
>
> "Yes, I am." I must explain that many good policemen stayed in their job during those times, so they could help Jews and political prisoners. This particular policeman had been on duty during the time when my father, with all his children, had to spend the night sitting on the floor of the police station.
>
> "I will never forget that night," the policeman told me. "It looked to me like it was a celebration instead of the beginning of so much suffering in prisons and concentration camps. I often tell people how your father was so calm, and how he read Psalm 91 to everyone."
>
> When my father was arrested, he was very old and weak. I do not believe that he would have lived very long, even if he had not been in prison. He was, after all, eighty-four years old. When we were arrested, he said to me, "Corrie, the best is yet to be," knowing that God had given him that assurance. For him, the best came ten days later, when he went to be with his Lord.

Jesus once said:

> In my Father's house are many mansions: if it were not so, I would have told you. I go to prepare a place for you.
>
> John 14:2

I remember Nollie telling me: "We love the Jews because we can thank them for the two greatest treasures. First of all, a Book written by Jews. It is the Bible and we must thank Israel for it. It is the Book which is almost bursting with good news and glorious promises. All its writers were Jews, except Luke, but he was converted through a Jew." I want to thank you, the Jews, for this Book. For the Bible has shown me the way to the second blessing which Nollie mentioned. It got me acquainted with my greatest Friend. He was a Jew. On His divine side He was the Son of God, but on His human side He was a Jew. And this Friend is my Saviour!

What a joy it has been for me to be in Jerusalem, the reunited city, now entirely in Israeli hands. However, we are all conscious of the fact that the times are very serious, not only in this country, but for the whole world. And what a joy that in this Book we see God's side of the history of the world. Many of you are expecting the Messiah to come, and so are we Christians. We believe He is coming again and He will do what He promised, "I will make all things new." Then the whole earth will be covered with the knowledge of the Lord like the waters cover the bottom of the sea.

Hallelujah, the best is yet to be!
I wish you Shalom, shalom, shalom!

Appendix

Casper ten Boom

May 18, 1859–March 10, 1944

It is not an easy thing to give a review of the life of such a greatly loved Haarlemmer in just a few pages. Suffice it therefore to give at the end of this article, without further comment, a list of the positions which he occupied during his lifetime; let that list speak for itself in indicating the extent to which he gave himself to the community, and let us limit ourselves principally in these few lines to his personality.

It can truly be said that, even after his death, he lives on for the many who worked with him or who had been in contact with him in any way at all. His optimism, his cordiality, his warm interest, and especially his strong faith, made it possible for him to be a blessing to many. Whenever one went to 19 Barteljorisstraat, one would meet new people who had come to ask Haarlem's "grand old gentleman" for help or advice, and he always spoke to them very kindly and never gave the impression that he was in a hurry. His home became an "oasis" for people in trouble who needed a refreshing word of encouragement. This was especially the case during the dark years of the war. In his house, countless people, especially Jews, found a hiding place from the relentless enemy. When anybody pointed out to him the great danger which threatened him night and day, he always answered quietly, "It will be an honor for me, if it is necessary, to die for God's chosen people, the Jews." These were not merely words. They were proved by his arrest which ended in his lonely death in prison. His death is tragic, but if he could still speak, he would point out to us that we must not keep looking at the tragic side of his death, because for him it meant entering into glory. Although he intensely enjoyed all the good things of this life, he knew that it was only transitory happiness. To use his own words, "The best is yet to be."

His life here has ended now, and it remains for us to be very thankful that we got to know this lovable man in so many different places (and he was himself, wherever he was). He will be an example to many for a long time.

BOB VAN WOERDEN

Positions which Mr. ten Boom occupied during his lifetime.

Cofounder and Chairman of Haarlem Christian Primary School Committee.

President/Commissioner of the Nassau Bank.

Chairman of the Dutch Committee for the Support of the White Cross colony in Java.

Vice-chairman, Department of Small Businesses, Chamber of Commerce and Factories, Haarlem.

Nestor (for seventeen years) of the Chamber of Commerce and Factories, Haarlem.

Chairman of the international organization of the "Union Horlogere" (Watchmakers Society).

Chairman of the Christian Tradespeople's Society, "Boaz" and Chairman of the Tradespeople's Central Council since 1923.

Committee member of Labor Council.

Committee member of the Christian Protestant Society for the Rehabilitation of Prisoners, Barteljorisstraat Society, and Anti-revolutionary Political Association.

Chairman of the Haarlem branch of the Dutch Watch-maker's Society.

Committee member of the Cooperative Purchase Society of Dutch Watchmakers.

Editor of the Watchmaker's magazine *Christiaan Huygens.*

Cofounder of the Haarlem volunteer civil guard.

Cofounder of Orange Nassau Institute. Haarlem Secondary School.

He wrote "Memories of an old watchmaker" and "The exact regulation of precision watches."

Mr. ten Boom was a Knight of the Order of Orange Nassau.

The International edition of the *Reader's Digest* made a condensed version of the book *The Hiding Place,* which tells the story of Casper ten Boom and his family. Before they did this, they went to Holland to obtain information on whether Mr. ten Boom really was a good watchmaker. It would be understandable that Corrie, his daughter, who loved him, thought that he was, but was he really? They went to the Dutch Association of Watchmakers and received this information: Casper ten Boom was known not only in Holland as a good watchmaker, but was also known internationally in a large part of Europe. He was called the best watchmaker in the Netherlands. He was a student of Hoü, in his time the best clockmaker in the world. His clock "the Hoü 2" can still be seen in Leiden.

Here is a translation of an old Haarlem newspaper clipping. The article was written by a local reporter and appeared under a photograph of Casper ten Boom.

Captured by our lens . . . Mr C. ten Boom.

Mr C. ten Boom is a very well-known personality in our

town, and not only in trade circles. He was born on 18th May, 1859 in Haarlem and has therefore now reached the age of seventy-five, though one would never guess it, seeing him walking through the streets of Haarlem. He was the recipient of many tokens of appreciation when he reached the age of seventy-five. He is respected in Haarlem as a worker for the interests of the tradespeople and also as an able watchmaker. He is Chairman of the Christian Tradespeople's Society, "Boaz" and member of the Tradespeople's Central Council for Haarlem and the surrounding area.

The esteem in which the other members of his trade hold Mr ten Boom can be seen in his Chairmanship of the Dutch branch of the "Union Horlogere" (Watchmakers' Society) and in the fact that he has been the editor of the Watchmakers' magazine, *Christiaan Huygens* for the last thirty years.

Mr ten Boom is the Nestor of the Chamber of Commerce. His patriarchal figure graces the Chairman's seat of that body once a year when the Chamber holds its first meeting of the year. When the meeting opens he makes one of his good, short speeches, always seasoned with humor, of which he knows the secret.

Mr ten Boom is an industrious, able and worthy man. Let us also state that he is a member of the electoral college of the Dutch Reformed Church.

You may write to Corrie ten Boom at Box 2040, Orange, CA 92669. Her magazine THE HIDING PLACE is published bi-monthly from the same address.